Sell Your Business for the Max!

Your Step-by-Step Planner for Profit, Success & Freedom

by **STEVE KAPLAN**

Workman Publishing ▪ New York

To every entrepreneur—for all the hard work
and sacrifices they have made to realize their dreams.

To Ryan and Madison—always aim high
and remember that if you work hard and believe in yourself
you can make all your dreams a reality.

Published simultaneously in Canada by Thomas Allen & Son Limited.

Library of Congress Cataloging-in-Publication Data is available.
ISBN 978-0-7611-4784-8

Workman books are available at special discounts when purchased in bulk for premiums and sales promotions as well as for fund-raising or educational use. Special editions or book excerpts also can be created to specification. For details, contact the Special Sales Director at the address below.

Design by Gary Montalvo

Workman Publishing Company, Inc.
225 Varick Street
New York, NY 10014-4381
www.workman.com

Printed in the United States of America
First printing January 2009

10 9 8 7 6 5 4 3 2 1

Contents

Preface v
Introduction: On the Brink 1

PART I **PREPARING FOR THE SALE**
1. Valuation 15
2. Select Your Team and Representative 27
3. Prepare Your Company 43
4. Identify Prospects 55

PART II **NEGOTIATING THE DEAL**
5. Ignite a Bidding War 67
6. Negotiate Effectively 73
7. Payout Structure and Currency 81
8. Do Due Diligence 91
9. Popping the Cork 107

PART III **GOING FOR THE LIMIT**
10. Get the Premium Price 113
11. Communicate Effectively 125
12. Protect Your Employees and Yourself 137
13. Plan for Succession 143

PART IV **FIVE KILLER MISTAKES**
14. The "Yak Yak" Factor 155
15. Invisibility 161
16. The "Yee Haw!" Factor 169
17. Deal Fatigue 175
18. The Sudden Stop 183
19. The Last Word 189

About the Author 191
Acknowledgments 193

Preface

SO THERE I WAS, just minding my own business, a happy guy building a marketing organization and focusing on sales. My company was doing great and I was lovin' life. Then one day a few things occurred to me:

- **How long would the good times last?** Business was good, growing year after year, and my clients were paying us hefty amounts to handle their businesses, but I knew that marketing, like any industry, is cyclical. How long would my run last before my customers decided to insource many of the services we were providing?
- **What would happen if I were out of the picture?** My business was kicking butt, with sales in excess of $30 million, but over 75 percent of the revenues were being brought in by me. Although this might speak well for my sales skills, it was terrible for the business. If I were sick or hurt and unable to work, everything I had built would vanish within a year.
- **Was I stuck here?** Although the business and money were great, I was ready to move on to new challenges. But I was selling all day, running the business at night, and helping raise my children in between; I had no time left over to even think about personal growth.
- **How long could I keep up the pace?** After fourteen straight years of eighty-hour weeks, I was starting to wonder.

My company had grown from a couple of employees to an organization with many services and processes. I was getting more and more big customers and leveraging my relationship with them to get deeper and deeper into their organizations. We were also developing more and more services to grow horizontally and vertically, first making sure the business was on solid footing and then building processes to handle the growth. Of course, these strategies hadn't been named yet, because writing the books about them—*Bag the Elephant* and *Be the Elephant*—was still in my future.

What future? At the rate I was going, my time was getting more and more swallowed up in running and growing my business. I asked myself, Is this really what I want to keep doing? Should I move on to new challenges? Could the business succeed without me? And even if I were still going strong, how long would the good times last? How long would we keep growing? What if we took a hit in the next business cycle?

These questions needed answering. And that's why I'm now sitting in a hotel room in Aspen, about to close on the mountain home I've always dreamed of, writing this preface for my third book. My subject? How to sell your company for maximum value.

For entrepreneurs, businesses are like children. You raise your business from infancy, see it through the early years of childhood, keep it from falling off cliffs during its adolescence, celebrate the triumphs of its early adulthood—and suddenly it's time for it to leave home and go out on its own. At least, that's the way it feels.

Like your offspring, your business may be a source of pride for you or a disappointment—and either way, it may motivate you to separate yourself from it. Your business may follow one of several paths:

- It may never get off the snail trail, failing to thrive and grow, causing you endless frustration. It may just be hanging by a thread, ready to fall in the slightest economic storm.
- It may grow to a certain size and then level off, enabling you to pay your bills and send the kids to college, but leaving you tired of the grind and wondering if there's something else out there for you.
- It may hit the elephant trail and thrive, evolving into a mature, healthy, large organization with processes in place and additional services developed and branded.

When the time comes, you'll know it: The urge grows in you to step aside and take your well-earned vacation from all that hard work, or simply to get out while the getting's good, while you still can and before the hard times arrive. I hear from many business owners who have read my first two books that they have achieved business success, but now would like to step aside, collect their rewards, and enjoy life for a while or move on to another project:

- "I've gotten feelers from another entity that might be interested in buying my business—yeeehaaaw!"
- "I'm always looking to sell my business so I can take a breath and do what I really love."
- "I want a bigger stage, and if I sell to the right company, I'll be doing more meaningful work."
- "I want to strike while the iron's hot, and the industry and business will never be better."

I hear from others who are in desperate straits and need to sell their companies quickly:

- "My business is going under and I need to sell while I have something to sell."
- "I'm financially screwed if I can't sell and get money back to family and friends who've invested with me."
- "I want off the treadmill. This business is killing me."

Whichever part of the necessity spectrum you're on, I'm writing this book for you. I'm filling it with stories that I've lived or been involved with—and, believe me, not all of them are good. This book will not only be about the mistakes others have made, but be about the things I did wrong, learned from, and eventually did right. This is the knowledge I want to pass along to you—the stuff I wish somebody had told me before I sold my first company. Let's call it hindsight in advance.

People ask me all the time what is the best thing about financial independence. Is it foreign sports cars? Luxury cruises to far corners of the globe? Lavish houses in exotic places? The answer for me is a simple one: freedom. It's the freedom to do what I want—consulting, public speaking, writing books—without the pressure of having to do anything at all.

Business is in my blood. I've always loved it, even in the early days when it was hard. I know what it's like to sweat out meeting a payroll or to sleep in a car while traveling because the $100 for a hotel room would be better spent on sales materials or a client lunch. But business is far more enjoyable now that I don't have to make a living from it. I can simply choose to do it because I like to.

In fact, even as I'm writing this, I'm negotiating to acquire a business in the mobile commerce industry, consulting several other businesses, helping to develop a new charitable foundation, and doing more business-consulting and public-speaking gigs.

But success takes a lot more than luck, especially when it comes to reaping the rewards of your work by selling your company. This is an especially tricky aspect of business. It's not something you do regularly; there's a good chance you've never sold a business before.

Whatever state your business is in, if you're considering selling now or later, this book will lead you through the essentials of the process. *Sell Your Business for the Max* is based on my vast experience of buying and selling businesses. It will tell you how to get your business ready to sell, when to start (now!), how to negotiate effectively, how to maximize the sell price, how to use your understanding of the sell process to your advantage, and much more. It will show you that the devil is in the details.

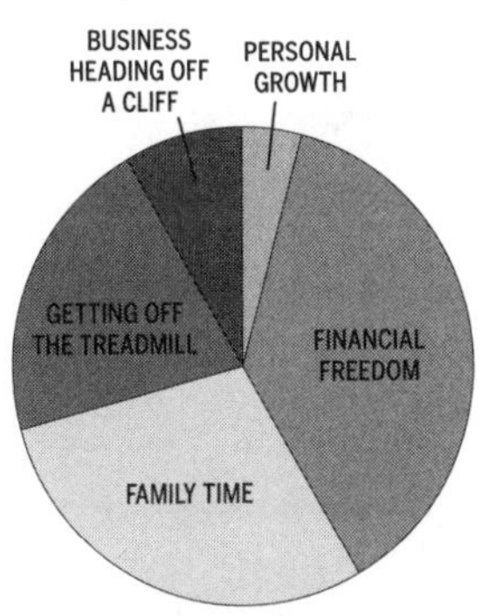

WHY BUSINESS OWNERS WANT TO SELL THEIR BUSINESSES

The information I share in this book is proprietary. I've developed it by utilizing knowledge I've garnered from the one-hundred-plus transactions I've been part of. The perspective you'll hear is unique and personal; it gives you the benefit of what I've learned, not only as a buyer and a seller, but as a player on the international stage as well. Although the tactics may vary, the strategies that work in the United States also work in Auckland, Buenos Aires, London, Toronto, Prague, and Shanghai. They work for businesses of all sizes—mom-and-pops, elephants, and everything between.

So let's get to it. You're poised on the brink of your ultimate goal: the big sale.

INTRODUCTION

On the Brink

OUR GOAL AS BUSINESS OWNERS IS TO SELL THE COMPANY. That's a pretty bold statement, isn't it? Your automatic response is, "Hey, I love owning this business. I get a kick out of being my own boss, running the enterprise, and making a lot of money. I could do this forever."

Nevertheless, it's true: About 98 percent of us want to get out of our business—some of us right away, the rest of us at some point in the future.

When the idea of selling your company comes to you—and if it hasn't already, it will—it arrives in one of three situations:

- You've reached a point in your life or career where you feel ready to move on to something new—a new business, new responsibilities, new creative endeavors, more time with your family—or perhaps just to get out from under the weight of your business and see what comes next. But you can't do it without leaving the business in someone else's hands. You think, maybe it's time to sell the company, take the money, and run.
- You're cruising along with no thought of anything except running and growing your business, preoccupied with the day-to-day tasks of keeping things moving along, either managing enormous profits or scratching to find more money to prop everything up, when suddenly you get a phone call, an e-mail, a letter, or a visit from someone who wants to discuss buying your company.
- You finally have a few minutes to yourself, you sit back, close your eyes, and all you can dream about are the riches coming your way from selling your business.

When you become conscious that selling the company is a possibility, you can be in any of several situations in terms of your business's health, ranging between two extremes:

- Your business may be prospering, growing, competing well, adding jobs and markets year after year, looking at blue skies—in which case the idea of an acquisition may well have occurred to the prospective buyer before it popped into your head, because there are always other companies on the lookout for quick ways to grow, and acquiring your company might be one of those ways.
- Your business may be crashing, its cash flow shriveling, profits shrinking, the economy nose-diving, causing you endless headaches with little prospect of the security you desire, and selling would be a quick way out of this everyday pressure cooker—in which case the idea of selling that popped into your head may not be matched by anybody else's wish to acquire you.

Whether your business is booming or in the dumps, your mandate is to sell it for as much as possible. The circumstance that promises you the best outcome is owning a business that's prospering and having someone else come to you with an offer. If your company is a moneymaker and you're not eager to sell, you're as alluring to a buyer as a shiny new lure is to a hungry largemouth bass, and you can probably count on getting top dollar if you don't get your line caught in the weeds. On the other hand, if you own a lagging company and are desperate to get rid of it, this scenario can send any possible trophy buyers in the lake swimming in the opposite direction.

At any rate, somewhere in the front or the back of your mind, you're thinking, yes, eventually I will sell. Maybe not today, maybe not next year, but on some auspicious day when I know I can get the maximum possible price, perhaps on that day I'll sell.

The only real questions that remain are, When *is* the best time to sell? When do the stars align to bring about the best opportunity to make that killing?

When the Stars Are Aligned

There's a big difference between wanting to sell and being ready to sell. The optimum time to sell a business is when the following four conditions occur simultaneously:

Business. The business is hitting on all cylinders. It's grown over the last three consecutive years, with this year's growth looking even better than last year's and the trend line curving up. The business is packaged for a sale with the necessary processes in place. Marketing materials have been developed to promote all the company's positives, and you've built an organization that can function without you.

Marketplace. Both your industry and complementary industries are growing, with consolidation in your industry at its height and trend data showing no signs of slowing.

Economy. The economy is thriving and economic indicators are trending up. Public companies are meeting their quarterly earnings numbers, and the stock market is stable and climbing. Your customers (businesses or consumers) have money to spend on your goods and services.

Personal. You've prepared yourself mentally for the sale. You understand the acquisition process, have a team of support experts in mind, can block out the time necessary to drive the effort, and have at least thought about what you might do if you or your buyer decides that you will not be involved in running the business post sale.

Now, here's the reality: The ideal situation never happens.

After involvement from both sides in more than one hundred acquisitions, I can tell you that conditions for a sale may be good or great, but they are never as good as you might wish them to be. Why? Because several of the key factors are beyond your control.

- The stars are almost never aligned.
- Even when the stars are aligned, you still may not get that max deal for your business.
- You can sell a business in any market if you know what to do, but you'll need the skills and knowledge garnered from years of experience.
- Even with skills and knowledge, selling a business isn't easy, and selling it for the max is even harder. It involves many activities, all interwoven and working in tandem, and it means avoiding miscues and missteps.

Throughout the years I've learned a thing or two about how to sell a business for the max. I know what separates success from failure, what differentiates businesses that sell for the max from businesses that don't sell or fail to reach their maximum price potential.

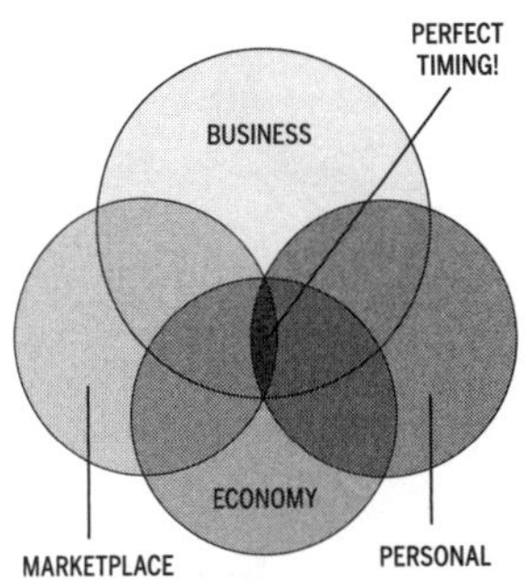

TIMING ISN'T EVERYTHING

You can still sell your business for big money even if you're not in the sweet spot. But try to get as many factors as you can.

Ten Steps to a Max Deal

To give your company its best shot at selling for the max, read and implement the following ten steps:

1. **Establish a baseline valuation.** Find out what your business is worth under several simple valuation models.

2. **Select your selling team.** Identify the capabilities needed and select people to fulfill them; decide whether you need or want representation.

3. **Prepare your business for the sale.** Whip it into shape; promote what's important to the buyer; learn how to position your business; create marketing materials that present your business in the proper light.

4. **Identify prospective buyers.** Where do they come from? How do you contact them and learn about them so that you can be effective in negotiating?

5. **Spark a bidding war.** Incite a competition to acquire your company by finding the right second prospect to make an offer.

6. **Negotiate effectively.** Understand the basis for the negotiation; prepare the playing field; know what roles you and others should play in the negotiations.

7. **Consider different deal structures.** Know the pros and cons of stock versus cash and up-front versus earn-out in different situations.

8. **Prepare for the diligence process.** Use it to your advantage to command a higher sell price; breeze through it by being prepared; exercise seller's due diligence on the buyer.

9. **Understand the close.** Don't get blindsided by the event; know what to expect.

10. **Sell through the roof.** Get the premium price by building a self-sustaining organization, knowing when and how to communicate effectively to customers and employees, and giving your employees post-sale security.

These steps are not to be taken in isolation; each works together with the others. Read the entire book, not just the parts that you feel are most relevant to you. For example, if you're trying to identify and communicate all the great value in your business, you'll find solid strategies for doing so in chapter 10, "Get the Premium Price"; however, to make those strategies work most effectively, you'll need to know how to use them in conjunction with other aspects of the sale process, such as exercising due diligence (chapter 8), creating great marketing materials (chapter 3), fomenting a bidding war (chapter 5), and communicating effectively (chapter 11).

Now, have you already received an offer and met with your prospective buyer, but your business is far from ready to sell because of the work still left to do in getting it in shape for the max price? Don't worry. You might have to pull a few late-nighters to whip it into shape, but it's important that you do so, and this book will help you do it. You'll find a ton of tips that you can use right away—but read the whole book first so you can see where those tips fit into the grand scheme of things.

To make the book easy to use, I've blocked out the steps in four distinct stages that follow the sale process more or less chronologically. Note, however, that certain aspects of the discussion, particularly in the part on getting the premium price, are important to know and use at all times, whether or not you're considering a sale: Effective communication, for example, or branding your "unique selling propositions" (USPs) for your customers and your employees.

- Steps 1–4 (chapters 1–4) cover activities you'll need to do before you begin talking with a prospect.
- Steps 5–9 (chapters 5–9) cover actions that take place after you've made contact with your prospective buyer.
- Step 10 is actually a four-part step (chapters 10–13) that will guide you through the secrets of turning a good sale into a max-value sale.

I've finished with five killer mistakes you'll need to avoid. Since I've made most of them at one time or another, I thought I'd share them with you in chapters 14–18 so you can be prepared in a way I wasn't.

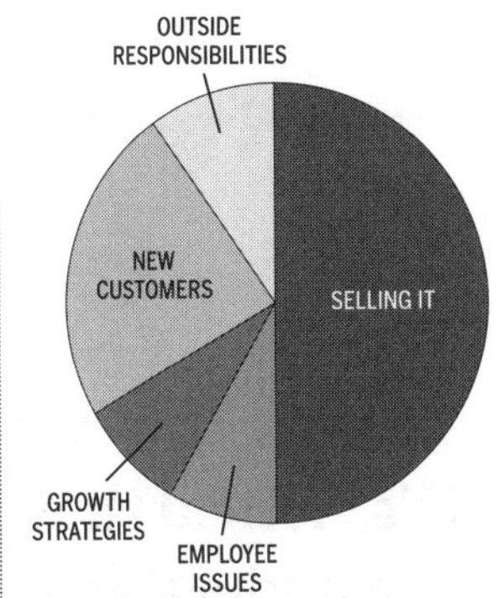

WHAT BUSINESS OWNERS SPEND TIME THINKING ABOUT

Most consider selling their company at least once a day.

Know Your Goals

Before you start down the life-altering path to selling your business, it's important to know why you're doing it and what you expect to gain from it. Is it money? Freedom? Leisure? Getting started on a new enterprise? When I sold one of my businesses, I was looking for a partner to help me grow my business faster than I could have alone, and I wanted a way to secure the future for myself and my employees.

It's critical that you understand specifically what you expect from a sale.

Have a look at the first worksheet in this section; give some thought to expressing your true motives. Do your best to put down on paper what you want to achieve by selling. Be specific. You will need to refer back to these objectives as you negotiate price and terms and progress toward closing the deal.

Then, if you think you're ready to start toward your goals, we'll jump right in with an assessment of where you stand now. Later we'll revisit this assessment and see how far you've advanced toward the goal of getting the maximum price for your company.

INTRODUCTION WORKSHEET

Your Goals and Objectives

Enumerate what you hope to achieve by selling your company. Be specific.

FINANCIAL GOALS (SALE PRICE)

PERSONAL GAIN FROM SALE (YOUR TAKE)

AMOUNT OF CASH INFUSION INTO THE BUSINESS (FROM BUYER)

GOALS FOR YOUR BUSINESS POST-SALE (GLOBAL, NEW TECHNOLOGY, ETC.)

GOALS FOR YOUR EMPLOYEES POST-SALE (INDIVIDUALLY OR AS A GROUP)

PERSONAL POST-SALE GOALS (STAY WITH BUSINESS, START A NEW BUSINESS, ETC.)

The Max Value Model (MVM) and the Max Value Quotient (MVQ)

The Max Value Model is a tool I developed for gauging how well prepared you are to sell your company for top value. It's designed to show sellers of any business, regardless of size, where their business stands. Does the business need work? Is it ready to be sold? Can it fetch a premium price?

Complete the Max Value Model now, before you get into the meat of the book, to get your baseline score and an idea of where you stand with respect to your best possible sale. As you proceed through the book and begin to prepare your business for the sale, revisit the MVM periodically to see how your Max Value Quotient is improving. By the end of the book, you'll be amazed at just how far your MVQ has risen.

1. Complete the MVM. Each of the statements has a weighted point value based on its importance to the max sale.
2. Add up your points to find your MVQ.
3. Check your MVQ against the key to see whether you're ready to sell your business for the max.

THE MAX VALUE MODEL (MVM)

Select the statement that best applies to you in each of the first two items.

VALUATION

1. You've run different valuations using different methods to determine the best one for you.	_______	10 pts
You've made your valuation based on another (comparable) acquisition in your industry.	_______	8 pts
You have a sell price in mind and it's based on a formula.	_______	4 pts
You have a sell price in mind but haven't based it on anything other than your expectations.	_______	2 pts
You haven't thought about a sell price.	_______	0 pts

SELECTING A TEAM AND REPRESENTATIVE

2. You've assembled a team or person(s) with the following expertise: Tax, accounting, legal, mentor.	_______	15 pts
You haven't identified a team member(s) for each of the capabilities but you plan to do so.	_______	10 pts
You're hiring a representative and staying out of the picture.	_______	2 pts
You're planning on handling all aspects of the deal by yourself.	_______	0 pts

For the remainder of the MVM, check yes or no for each item. Give yourself zero points for each No answer and the appropriate value for each Yes.

	YES	NO
BUSINESS SHAPE—PACKAGED TO SELL		
3. You have written a general background: Company history, summary of services, business strategy, core competencies (things you do best).	_____ 5	_____ 0 pts
4. You have completed a written description of services: Detailed overview of products and services, business units, benefits to customers, growth strategy.	_____ 5	_____ 0 pts
5. You have identified your customers: Customer growth, list of clients, repeat customers, customer programs, case studies.	_____ 5	_____ 0 pts
6. You have defined operations: Flow chart, how you operate your company, overview of processes in place to facilitate efficient operation.	_____ 5	_____ 0 pts
7. You have established and documented your information systems: Overview, databases, expansion, capabilities.	_____ 5	_____ 0 pts
8. You have outlined your management and employees: Organization chart, compensation philosophy.	_____ 5	_____ 0 pts
9. You have examined your financial performance: Overview, charts of past three years plus upcoming year estimate, revenue, gross margin, income, EBITDA (earnings before interest, taxes, depreciation, and amortization), year-over-year growth rates.	_____ 5	_____ 0 pts
10. You have used charts and graphs to highlight value areas in the business.	_____ 5	_____ 0 pts
11. You have shored up your accounting and you have prior three years' financial statements and three-year projections at the ready, showing consistent growth trends.	_____ 15	_____ 0 pts
IDENTIFYING PROSPECTS		
12. You've analyzed the market to come up with a list of prospects.	_____ 5	_____ 0 pts
13. You've considered industry, financial, and complementary buyers.	_____ 5	_____ 0 pts
14. You have a list of at least ten viable prospects.	_____ 10	_____ 0 pts

THE BIDDING WAR

15. You've received inquiries within the past year from more than one prospect. ______ 10 ______ 0 pts

NEGOTIATING EFFECTIVELY

16. You or your team member has successfully negotiated a sale or understands how valuation formulas relate to negotiations and how to leverage your business strengths. ______ 10 ______ 0 pts

DEAL STRUCTURE AND CURRENCY

17. You understand the pros and cons and are willing to accept stock as payment instead of cash. ______ 10 ______ 0 pts

18. Your business is poised for growth, so you understand an earn-out and are open to one. ______ 10 ______ 0 pts

DILIGENCE

19. You have many of the items requested by a buyer at the ready (see "Seller's Due Diligence List," chapter 8). ______ 10 ______ 0 pts

20. You're planning to create a data room with all materials for the buyer's review. ______ 10 ______ 0 pts

THE CLOSE

21. You're planning to personally review all closing documents before the closing. ______ 5 ______ 0 pts

22. You understand the concept of representations and warranties made in a deal. ______ 5 ______ 0 pts

THROUGH THE ROOF

23. You've identified and branded many processes and unique selling propositions to create value throughout your business. ______ 15 ______ 0 pts

24. You've developed a formal succession plan. ______ 10 ______ 0 pts

25. You've considered and mapped out what you want for yourself post deal with respect to stock options, bonus pools, and other employment issues. ______ 5 ______ 0 pts

26. You've considered your valuable employees and made moves to keep them working in your business through employment agreements, with bonus pools to keep their motivation high in order to drive the business hard during earn-out periods. ______ 5 ______ 0 pts

MISCELLANEOUS

27. You personally have sold a business before. ______ 10 ______ 0 pts
28. You have a mentor with experience in selling two or more businesses. ______ 10 ______ 0 pts
29. You're planning to stay with the business for at least one year post-sale. ______ 10 ______ 0 pts
30. You have full time to dedicate to the sale process without your business suffering at all. ______ 10 ______ 0 pts

YOUR MAX VALUE QUOTIENT: ____________ total pts

MAX VALUE QUOTIENT KEY

If your MVQ was 225–250, *you are ready to proceed and are in a great position to max out on a sale of your business. Read the book and proceed with your sale.*

If your MVQ was 200–224, *you're not quite there, but you're close. Your business is well prepared and you should do well, but strive to get additional points to break the 225 threshold. Read the book, then pick up a couple more points by implementing some of the material discussed.*

If your MVQ was 150–199, *you're not ready for the max sale. You might have enough here to get a sale, but you need to use the model to shape your business and make it more sell ready. Read the book closely, implement all the strategies, take the MVM again, then gauge your readiness by adding up your new MVQ. Proceed with the sale only when you are close to the 225 mark.*

If your MVQ was 149 or less, *the business definitely isn't ready yet for a sale of any kind. You need to read the book carefully and implement the suggestions. This will move your business up the ranking until you reach the 225 mark.*

PART ONE

Preparing for the Sale

...

CHAPTER ONE
Valuation
Page 15

CHAPTER TWO
Select Your Team and Representative
Page 27

CHAPTER THREE
Prepare Your Company
Page 43

CHAPTER FOUR
Identify Prospects
Page 55

CHAPTER 1

Valuation

SO YOU'VE DECIDED TO SELL YOUR COMPANY. Now the fun begins. How realistic are those fantasies of the riches selling your business will bring? Will you really be able to retire? Is that new house in the country likely to happen? What about your plans to start that charity you've been dreaming of and become a celebrated philanthropist? Will there be enough money to make a run at it?

The answer to all these questions is yes—*if* you can sell your business for enough money.

What is your company worth? I have one simple rule: A company is worth exactly what someone will pay for it at the time of the sale—not a penny more, not a penny less. The same company and buyer might have a different valuation in a different market or under different circumstances.

Sometimes a buyer will offer more than what you believe to be the fair value, and sometimes less. In most cases, the seller and the buyer independently develop their own valuations. However, the buyer typically submits an offer or term sheet proposing the general deal points, including an initial offer and how the buyer arrived at that offer. If you are approached by a prospective buyer about

Valuation is simply what your company is worth at a given time. Often this is also the proposed selling or offer price of your company. Valuation can also be thought of as the battleground where you and the buyer negotiate the price. There are several ways to derive valuation, so even in the choosing of a valuation model, you're in a negotiation. Are you ready?

buying your business, simply ask the buyer to send you a term sheet. This will give you something in writing to address. The prospective buyer might wish to see a set of financials, or at least discuss them with you, to help the buyer formulate its offer. Don't make the mistake of thinking that a term sheet is binding; it's not. There will always be an escape clause for the buyer, such as "pending diligence" or even the explicit statement "This is a non-binding offer." Remember, your business isn't sold until you have actually received payment.

If you are approached by a prospective buyer, simply ask the buyer to send you a term sheet. This will give you something in writing to address.

There are several methods of determining your company's value, and these can produce different valuations for the same company. As you would expect, the seller's valuation is typically higher than the buyer's; negotiations then follow to close the gap. If the buyer's valuation comes in higher than the seller's, a deal can usually be completed quickly. (But don't count on this happening.)

Perhaps the most common method of valuation is for the buyer to offer a multiple of your average yearly earnings, based on your current year, the past two to three years, and one or more future years' projections. Another buyer might offer a multiple of your cash flow, or even a benchmarked valuation based on previous comparable transactions in your industry, such as a percent of sales.

No matter the method of determining your company's value, you can push that figure upward by showing a history of strong growth and by ensuring future growth. To accomplish this difficult task, you must not neglect your current operations during the selling process, for to do so might result in a profit hiccup that could cost you big dollars on the sale. This is important. Don't shift gears from running your company to selling it; you must somehow manage to do the latter without compromising the former. (There's more on this in chapter 16, "The 'Yee Haw!' Factor," and elsewhere.)

You might also consider using an outside company to put together an independent valuation. This can be helpful, but in order to do the job right, the outside company will need the same information as you would if you were doing it yourself.

When selling a business, I develop an overall valuation for the company using three distinct models for determining value:

- Economic value
- Comparable value
- Emotional value

Now, I'm guessing that you hate the drudgery of finance and accounting as much as I do, but I've got to tell you—there's something about the opportunity for riches that makes this work a little more palatable. Anyway, you should use your accountant's expertise during this process, so you won't have to do too much of the math yourself. If you decide to use a financial representative, let her handle the valuation. (See chapter 2 for more on selecting your selling team.)

Economic Value

Economic value is based strictly on the numbers. It is determined by taking a profit or sales number and multiplying it by some factor. I use a simple two-step method for determining economic value:

1. **Calculate the average earnings before interest, taxes, depreciation, and amortization (EBITDA) over a five-year period:** the past two years, this year's projection, and the projected earnings for the next two years. Before you calculate the averages, make sure to add back dollars that wouldn't be deducted from the business if you hadn't owned it. For example, if you take an unusually large salary each year because you're the owner, add back to the profits each year the difference between the salary you took and what a fair salary would be for someone else to run the business. Other add-backs might include expenditures that will stop after a new owner comes in,

Here is an example of what the economic valuation might be for company ABC:

ABC COMPANY

	2 Years Ago	Last Year	This Year	Next Year	Year 2
EBITDA (earnings before interest, taxes, depreciation, and amortization)	$500,000	$600,000	$750,000	$900,000	$1,000,000
Add-backs:					
Salary adjustment	$30,000	$50,000	$80,000	$90,000	$90,000
Excess benefits	$7,000	$7,000	$9,000	0	0
Excess travel and entertainment	$20,000	$8,000	$5,000	0	0
Net adjusted earnings	$557,000	$665,000	$844,000	$990,000	$1,090,000

Average net adjusted earnings: $829,200 (5-year average)
Multiple for industry: 8×
Valuation based on economic value: $6,633,600 (8 × $829,200)

such as unusually high travel and entertainment expenses, huge profit-sharing contributions, or even the cost of company cars. Add-backs can be critical to yielding a much larger valuation. If you consider the fact that valuation is a multiple on each dollar sent to the bottom line, then each additional dollar could result in anywhere from $5 to $10 or even $15 more in valuation. If your business had averaged $50,000 a year in add-backs for four years and the valuation was set at earnings times 7, this could yield an additional $350,000 ($50,000 × 7) in your selling price.

Every business is different; be flexible in how you set your company's value. If you had a particularly poor year two years ago, start your averaging with last year; if you expect a huge year two years down the road, extend the averaging an extra year.

2. **Multiply the average earnings by a factor relevant to the industry.** For example, marketing and database companies might sell for anywhere between 6 and 14 times profit, whereas a quick-print business might sell at 3 to 4 times profit. This has to do mainly with profit margins being high in database and marketing and low in commodities such as printing.

Determining the right multiple is important. If you go too low, your valuation will leave money on the table; too high, and you might scare off a solid prospect. Outside valuation companies typically use economic valuation as their formula, but they do look at comparison data as well. The following discussion on comparable value includes some resources that will help you make the right decision for your industry.

Comparable Value

Comparable value weighs the historical purchase prices of companies similar to yours and the formulas used for valuation. Even if your business is a private company, you'll find information on public companies to be useful. The Securities and Exchange Commission (SEC) requires all public companies to file certain documents, which are available to everyone.

The two filings most helpful in supplying information on recent acquisitions are the 10-K and the 10-Q filings. Filed no later than ninety days after the end of the period, which in most cases is the end of the year, 10-Ks disclose details behind mergers and acquisitions. 10-Qs provide similar information but on a more current time frame, within forty-five days after the end of the period or quarter. Look for companies in your industry, specifically those that you know have purchased businesses similar to yours. You can access a vast store of information online through Yahoo, Google, *moneycentral .msn.com,* and other financial search engines and sites.

First, follow the links to ferret out information on acquisitions in your industry. You will find material acquisitions, including company names and sell price. Next, search the company that was acquired. I looked up the advertising industry and discovered that the media conglomerate WPP purchased 24/7 Real Media for $649 million. A search of the 24/7 Real Media website under News & Events provided more details on the transaction, including pricing, strategic fit for both companies, and more.

Even if your prospect isn't a public company, knowing your industry strengthens your negotiating position.

Second, back on your browser's home page, click on the Finance link, locate the public company by its call letters, click on SEC Filings, then the document of choice—10-K, 10-Q, or other. Review the mergers and acquisitions details, including the notes.

Also available are paid Internet subscription services, such as EDGAR Online and Hoovers.com, which can be helpful.

Another method of obtaining information on comparables is to hire someone who specializes in representing sellers of companies, as discussed in chapter 2, "Select Your Team and Representative." Still another way is to contact individuals who have sold businesses in your industry and simply ask them for advice. You'll be amazed at just how helpful these people will be.

If you're thinking of selling, get to know your comparables. This is especially important when your prospective buyer is a public company. The prospect will use comparables to benchmark your company and will probably base its offer on them. As a "public company, it will need to explain to its stockholders why it made the acquisition and why your company is worth the price it paid. Knowing your industry comparables enables you to negotiate with your eyes open; you can set your starting price at the high end of the comparable range, or even higher than any of your peers, if you can formulate reasons why your company is worth more. Even if your prospect isn't a public company, knowing your industry strengthens your negotiating position.

Emotional Value

Emotional value quantifies your emotional needs—that is, what you personally want to get for the company. This value takes into account your goals and objectives, which might range all the way from wanting to be a millionaire to simply

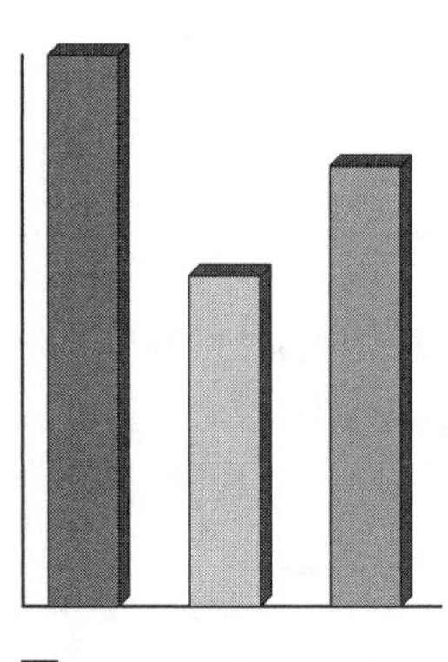

VALUE IS IN THE EYE OF THE BEHOLDER

Every business owner attaches an emotional valuation to the company. The key is making a buyer see what you see.

wanting to get out of debt. Although the emotional value of your company to you doesn't play a role in the buyer's offer, it will be pivotal in your negotiations by giving you perspective on what was important to you when you began the selling process. (Check the objectives you set in the Introduction.)

Your business's emotional value is of no interest to the buyer. If you're using this method of valuation, you'll have to show the buyer other reasons for considering it—that is, you'll need to create a formula that gets you logically to the emotional value you're seeking, working backward from the desired outcome to the opening of the sell process. I call this process "rationalizing the emotional."

Start with the amount you wish to get for the company, then find a formula that will get you there. For example, if you want to sell your company for $500,000 and your average profits from the last two years were $100,000, one possible formula could be five times the average profits from the last two years. Check the formula and amount you come up with against comparable and economic value to determine if it is a reasonable valuation.

Another factor to consider is upside value, the additional opportunity provided by your business to the prospect's company. It includes the opportunity for the buyer to increase its sales by acquiring your customer base, distribution channels, or products; the degree to which your sales and profits will improve the buyer's operating margin; and any components or processes that might reduce the buyer's costs or increase its margin.

Seek to get this upside value included in the valuation regardless of whether you're using an economic, comparable, or emotional valuation model, but understand that most buyers will object, claiming that the upside potential comes from the nature of their business rather than yours (in truth, it's a fortuitous meshing of the two). However, even if this doesn't end up yielding more hard dollars for you, simply discussing these opportunities makes a strong negotiating point and can help close the deal. At the very least, these upside value points should help drive the rationale for you to be getting the high end of the valuation range; if the buyer is considering a range of four to seven times average profits, the upside value should allow you to settle on or near the seven times multiple.

Use the worksheets below to derive your valuation so that you know what ballpark you're in; then move on to chapter 2. (See *www.stevekaplanlive.com/freebies* for simple valuation tools and calculators.)

WORKSHEET 1A

Company Projections

Since economic value is based solely on the numbers, it's important to calculate your economic value using several formulas so that you can identify the best one for you and your business situation.

Complete the following table, then calculate the various economic value options below. If you don't know these initial financial numbers, ask your accountant for some help. You should have financial projections for at least two years ahead. If you don't, stop and put them together; you'll need them when you make contact with a potential buyer. If you have Year 3 projections done, include these as well. These valuation methods are not set in stone; you are free to play with the various averages to see what works for you.

	2 Years Ago (Yr –2)	**Last Year (Yr –1)**	**This Year Projected (Yr 0)**	**Next Year Projected (Yr +1)**	**Two Years Projected (Yr +2)**
1. Total revenue/ sales	$ ________	$ ________	$ ________	$ ________	$ ________
2. EBITDA	________	________	________	________	________
3a. Add-backs:					
Excess owner compensation	________	________	________	________	________
Excess travel and entertainment	________	________	________	________	________
Other	________	________	________	________	________
Other	________	________	________	________	________
Other	________	________	________	________	________
3b. Total add-backs	________	________	________	________	________
4. Net adjusted earnings (2 + 3b)	$ ________	$ ________	$ ________	$ ________	$ ________

WORKSHEET 1B

Economic Valuation

Use the data derived in Worksheet 1A and select one of the three business scenarios most relevant to you.

SCENARIO A: IF YOUR BUSINESS IS GROWING

Weight your valuation toward future earnings, but bear in mind that if you end up with an earn-out over time, you'll have to perform to get the big payoff.

EARNINGS MULTIPLE

5. Four-year earnings average (0.25 × total of Yr –1 through Yr +2, line 4) $ ________
6. Industry multiple (range) on earnings (see page 24) ________ × to ________ ×
7. Valuation (line 5 × top multiple from line 6) $ ________

SALES MULTIPLE

8. Four-year revenue/sales average (0.25 × total of Yr –1 through Yr +2, line 1) $ ________
9. Industry multiple (range) on sales (see page 24) ________ × to ________ ×
10. Valuation (line 8 × top multiple from line 9) $ ________

SCENARIO B: IF YOUR BUSINESS IS STAGNANT

Spread the valuation across more historical years and fewer projected years. This will give the buyer comfort that you aren't front loading your valuation; it doesn't really matter to you, because your business is pretty much the same year to year.

EARNINGS MULTIPLE

11. Four-year earnings average (0.25 × total of Yr –2 through Yr +1, line 4) $ ________
12. Industry multiple (range) on earnings (see page 24) ________ × to ________ ×
13. Valuation (line 11 × top multiple from line 12) $ ________

SALES MULTIPLE

14. Four-year revenue/sales average (0.25 × total of Yr –2 through Yr +1, line 1) $ ________
15. Industry multiple (range) on sales (see page 24) ________ × to ________ ×
16. Valuation (line 14 × top multiple from line 15) $ ________

WORKSHEET 1B

Economic Valuation (Cont.)

SCENARIO C: IF YOUR BUSINESS IS SHRINKING

If your business is dropping off, you'll want to be paid more on past performance. Weight your average toward prior years. Your rationale? You're providing actual numbers, not projections, which the buyer will often discount on the assumption that the seller may have inflated them.

EARNINGS MULTIPLE

17. Three-year earnings average (0.33 × total of Yr –2 through Yr 0, line 4) $ ____________

18. Industry multiple (range) on earnings (see page 25) ______ × to ______ ×

19. Valuation (line 17 × top multiple from line 18) $ ____________

SALES MULTIPLE

20. Three-year sales average (0.33 × total of Yr –2 through Yr 0, line 1) $ ____________

21. Industry multiple (range) on sales (see page 25) ______ × to ______ ×

22. Valuation (line 20 × top multiple from line 21) $ ____________

WORKSHEET 1C

Comparable Valuation

INDUSTRY ______________________________

COMPARABLE 1

Buyer (company) ______________________________

Seller (company) ______________________________

Sell Price $ ______________

	Current	Last Year	Two Years Ago
Seller's revenues	$ ________	$ ________	$ ________
Seller's earnings (history)	$ ________	$ ________	$ ________

Formula for valuation ______________________________

Strategic fit ______________________________

Your valuation using Comparable 1 method $ ______________

COMPARABLE 2

Buyer (company) ______________________________

Seller (company) ______________________________

Sell Price $ ______________

	Current	Last Year	Two Years Ago
Seller's revenues	$ ________	$ ________	$ ________
Seller's earnings (history)	$ ________	$ ________	$ ________

Formula for valuation ______________________________

Strategic fit ______________________________

Your valuation using Comparable 2 method $ ______________

COMPARABLE 3

Buyer (company) ______________________________

Seller (company) ______________________________

Sell Price $ ______________

	Current	Last Year	Two Years Ago
Seller's revenues	$ ________	$ ________	$ ________
Seller's earnings (history)	$ ________	$ ________	$ ________

Formula for valuation ______________________________

Strategic fit ______________________________

Your valuation using Comparable 3 method $ ______________

Select the best valuation for your business from above $ ______________

List rationale for the valuation by mirroring from select comparable strategic fit:

____

UPSIDE VALUE
For each scenario, add the upside value to the formula. Even if you don't get credit for it, identifying it can help you get to the upper end of the multiple range.

Rationalizing the Emotional

To rationalize the emotional value of your company you need a good formula.

But how do you arrive at one? First, take your desired sale price and then reverse engineer the formulas used in Worksheet 1B. Decide which category your business falls into (growing, stagnant, or shrinking) and then convert your emotional multiple into an economic one.

You'll also have to compare multiples to industry comparable but use common sense. Prospective buyers will certainly pay a higher multiple on earnings than they would on sales, but determine what's right for you. Typically a buyer wouldn't pay 25X earning or 3X sales for a business so you might have to try other financial combinations or revise your expectations.

In the simplest terms:

Desired amount / Best business performance options = Economic valuation

Once you have the formula that makes sense and can rationalize your emotional sale price you are ready to counter a potential buyer's offer.

For example:

Desired amount from the sale: $ 5,000,000

Assuming business is stagnant:

Desired Amount	/	Avg. Sales	=	Sales Multiple
$ 5,000,000	/	$ 2,300,000		2.2X
Desired Amount	/	Avg. Income	=	Earnings Multiple
$ 5,000,000	/	$360,000		13.9X

Both the sales and the income multiples are a bit on the high side—particularly the sales multiple—but you now have a range. If you can position the business, identify and communicate all of the value in the business and put the seller at ease by following the steps in this book, you will have a real opportunity to get as close to your emotional value of the company as possible.

GROWING

Desired Amount	/	Avg. Sales	=	Sales Multiple
____________	/	______________	=	______X
Desired Amount	/	Avg. Sales	=	Earnings Multiple
____________	/	______________	=	______X

STAGNANT

Desired Amount	/	Avg. Sales	=	Sales Multiple
____________	/	______________	=	______X
Desired Amount	/	Avg. Sales	=	Earnings Multiple
____________	/	______________	=	______X

SHRINKING

Desired Amount	/	Avg. Sales	=	Sales Multiple
____________	/	______________	=	______X
Desired Amount	/	Avg. Sales	=	Earnings Multiple
____________	/	______________	=	______X

CHAPTER 2

Select Your Team and Representative

THERE'S AN OLD SAYING IN THE LEGAL PROFESSION: Anyone who acts as his own lawyer in a court of law has a fool for a client. I think a similar principle applies when you're selling your business. Now, I'm not going to say no one's ever done it successfully, but if you want to get the best deal, you'd be well advised to get some expert help, preferably in the form of a *team* of dedicated players who will do the legwork and support you at every turn. It's a scary, dangerous world out there if you're on your own with no experience.

Much of the work will be done, of course, by the buyer, who is not interested in buying a pig in a poke, and so will do heavy research on your business and its management to learn as much as possible about what makes it tick. But that still leaves a ton of work for you to do. So, before you even start the deal-making, you need to put together a team of trusted advisers who have the knowledge and experience to guide you around the potholes and pitfalls. You never want to get into a situation where the buyer knows more about your business and its potential than you do, or to be outmaneuvered by a buyer who knows more about buying than you do about selling. So get yourself a strong team.

AREAS OF EXPERTISE NEEDED

Ideally, your team will have the following specialists:

- *Tax adviser*
- *Accountant*
- *Financial planning adviser*
- *Attorney*
- *Mentor*
- *Representative or agent*
- *Others as needed for your specific industry*

Assembling Your Team

As you read through the discussion below, use Worksheet 2A at the end of this chapter to help you along. Map out the whole team so you can see that all the necessary areas of expertise are covered. Will the people you're thinking of selecting work together well? Are there conflicts of interest? Potential personality conflicts? Overlaps? Areas that aren't covered? Are there enough people to do the work? You need to see the overall picture and judge how your team will function before you call people and ask them to participate. Make adjustments as necessary to avoid aggravation later.

Rank your choices in order of preference, but keep this listing confidential; no one likes to know he's your second or third choice. Remember that if you assign people to multiple roles, your top choice in one area may be your second or third choice in another. Seek referrals from those you trust and make sure you're comfortable with all team members before signing them on. Ideally you'll have key management people as team members, but it's not fatal if you don't.

This team will be active throughout the process, especially in the discovery or diligence phase when the buyer seeks to learn all about your business (see chapter 8 for more on this phase). During this period, you might decide to develop a separate "diligence team" with more management members to address the specific business issues.

Spring for a dinner or lunch and have the whole team meet in advance to get everyone on the same page. Urge them to work together to produce the best outcome possible. For example, your accountant, tax specialist, and lawyer should join forces with you to create and explain the most favorable deal structure for you.

Remember that you'll probably have competing agendas; sometimes your business's needs will conflict with your own. When seeking advice from your chosen experts, ask for both perspectives.

Regardless of the magnitude of the deal, the following are capabilities you need on your team. Depending on your situation, you might choose to retain expertise or simply call in a few favors from experienced people you know. I can't even tell you how many calls I receive from friends and associates asking for a little help in reviewing a deal structure or just general advice. If I have the time,

I'm always willing to help, and I think you'll find the same to be true in your circle. People generally like to help other people.

In addition to the people discussed here, you might consider hiring a financial representative or agent (see page 33). I can think of plenty of times when this is a great way to go—just be sure it's the right agent and right situation.

Finally, even if you have a very small company, don't be intimidated by the depth of expertise outlined here. You will need guidance in the same areas as larger companies; the only difference between acquisitions involving huge companies and those involving small businesses is the caliber of the experts. Huge companies hire the big accounting firms, fancy consultants, and expensive law firms; smaller businesses might need to be more creative in getting their expertise and advice. Having been on both sides of this coin, I know that a smaller company can do even better than a larger company if it has the right expertise on its team.

Tax Adviser

Selling a company is a major tax event with potentially staggering effects. Having a good tax expert on your team can actually save you millions; it has done so for me, several times. I now include my tax expert in almost every investment decision I make. I strongly recommend that you do the same.

This might be the time to branch out beyond the one-person local CPA firm that has been preparing your income taxes. The laws are complex and in constant flux. Although you must satisfy your obligations to the government, you also need to maximize your wealth within the confines of the law. Look for a tax specialist, such as a tax attorney who handles estate planning. An all-purpose lawyer without tax expertise usually doesn't cut it. If your company accountant is a tax expert, you may not need outside help. If he is also your personal tax expert, that's okay, but unless I'm completely comfortable with him, I always prefer to separate personal and business, especially during a sale, when potentially large dollar amounts are flying around. You should make your personal tax accountant part of the team.

At most, 1 out of 5 deals I've seen utilize a team approach, leaving the seller vulnerable.

Coupling estate planning with wealth preservation may let you capitalize on some solid opportunities; you need someone on your team to explain these options to you. This might be the time to establish a trust. If you are being paid in the buyer's stock, you might give some of it to your children, set up a trust for your grandchildren, start that charity foundation you've been thinking about, or pursue other options. The opportunities are all around you.

Accountant

An accountant can help you do two essential things before the sale: (1) make sure your financials are buttoned up and accurate, and (2) develop financial reports requested by you or the prospect. You'll be monitoring the business even more closely than usual during the selling process and will need up-to-the-minute information quickly. If your accounting is done in-house—through a CFO, comptroller, or certified accountant, for example—that's okay; but if your accountant is more a bookkeeper than a fully qualified corporate accountant, you should give serious thought to hiring an outside accountant for the sale.

Your accountant should be able to walk potential buyers through the statements. This not only reassures the buyer, it adds a buffer between you and the buyer. You're still responsible for the numbers on the paper, of course, but a good accountant will put the buyer at ease with her knowledge of accountancy, so that the buyer is comfortable with the numbers you present.

Make it clear to your people that all requests for financial information from your prospect must be brought to your attention.

In any case, you need to limit access and filter the communication between this employee and the buyer. The two should *never* talk outside your presence. If there are problems, the explanation should come from you, not secondhand from one of your employees; more deals blow up because of loose talk from a finance employee than for almost any other reason. Make it clear to your people that all requests for financial information from your prospect must be brought to your attention. You don't want the prospect getting reports or information directly from your accountant; you need to screen and approve them first.

There's another reason to keep an eye on this interaction. Many buyers will seek to control the company they just acquired through the accounting and finance departments, reasoning that whoever controls the spending and budgeting essentially runs the business. Protect your employee by staying with him; you don't want to put him in a position of having to choose between being loyal to his current boss—you—and pleasing his future boss who might ask for some inside information.

Tell the prospect to run all requests through a central contact so that you can provide exactly what the prospect needs as quickly as possible. Let the prospect know that you need to manage your employees' priorities so they stay focused on the business. Most buyers understand this and will not complain.

Financial Planning Adviser

If things go well, you'll be coming into a lot of money. Are you sure you're ready? Beyond tax matters, you'll need someone to help you manage your wealth. That's why you'll need a financial planning adviser on your team—someone to help you keep track of your personal stake in the outcome, as opposed to other team members who are looking out for your company. Have your financial adviser on board before you sail into the stormy seas of selling your company.

A good financial planner will profile your goals and risk tolerance before recommending any investment strategy or other action. He will also be able to provide insights about your industry, including recent acquisitions, potential buyers, and more, at no cost (see chapter 4, "Identify Prospects").

The best way to find a personal financial adviser is through referrals. Get several, and check them out carefully. Although many people believe that big financial institutions are interested only in millionaires, that isn't the case. Once an institution hears you're considering selling your business, its interest will be piqued and it will be more than happy to assist. As a rule, larger firms have access to more financial products and provide more investment opportunities than do smaller firms—but in the end, it's the individuals who work with you, not the institutions they work for, who make the difference.

Attorney

You'll need good legal advice for several reasons. For your personal needs, you need an attorney to create and register new entities for estate planning or a stock sale. For your business, you need lawyers to update your corporate minutes book, review the purchase agreement, decipher details of any offers, point out potential risks, assess a buyer's creditworthiness, ensure compliance with regulatory requirements, review employment agreements, assess and act on profit-sharing plans, and register trademarks when necessary for your processes and unique selling propositions (as discussed in chapter 3, "Prepare Your Company"), among other reasons.

Ideally, you can retain a corporate attorney with a tax focus to perform these tasks for you, which amounts to one-stop shopping. Many good firms have several capabilities, and your point attorney can bring in other expertise within the firm as needed. The important thing, however, is to have the expertise at hand, so don't sacrifice expertise for convenience.

Mentor

Good mentoring is the scarcest and perhaps most important resource of all. That's why I wrote this book—to serve as your virtual mentor throughout your selling experience. But for sheer responsiveness and support, there's no substitute for a real mentor who can be there in person for you. Look for a mentor who has sold at least one business, who has no vested interest in your company, and who's motivated only by what's best for you. An experienced businessperson who can guide you through the sell process, tell you what's around the next corner, provide another perspective on your best interests, and help you rein in your misgivings is worth his or her weight in gold.

The mentor you should seek is one who doesn't need the money—in fact, one who has successfully sold a business and wants to help others do the same. Nevertheless, if you ask for things that require extra work or investment, such as researching a company or traveling, you should pay for the mentor's extra time or travel expenses.

The mentor you should seek is one who doesn't need the money—ideally, one who has successfully sold a business and wants to help others do the same.

How do you find a mentor? People you know, or mentors who come by personal referral from people you trust, are usually best. Most of us know someone successful, or someone who knows someone successful, in business. If you don't know the person directly, ask for an introduction, then set up a meeting. Ask your family, friends, associates, even the other potential team members, if they know of someone who can answer your questions and give you some pointers. Check industry publications, newspapers, and the Web to see who has recently sold businesses.

When you identify a potential mentor, call and ask for a meeting over breakfast or lunch. Start with a few questions about what to expect and what to be on guard for; see if a rapport develops between you. Is this person helpful and forthcoming? Does he seem eager to help you? Was selling his business a positive experience, or were there problems and regrets? Check him out on the Web; just because he sold his business doesn't automatically mean he did it right.

I've been on both sides of the table. I've called people to ask for advice, I've been called by others and asked to help—and I've enjoyed both mentoring and being mentored. But keep in mind that a mentor is not at all the same thing as a consultant. I'm not a big fan of hiring firms to create formal business plans, growth plans, overviews, or business models. Why? Because

1. It's your business, and you should have long since done the modeling and planning; if not, do so immediately—not just for the sale, but for the sake of the business. Have your managers, or others in the company, prepare their parts of the documents. (I'll walk you through what to put in your business overview in chapter 3, "Prepare Your Company.")

2. The documents will be from the consultant's perspective, not your own. Since you are the one doing the selling, you'll have to learn about your business all over again from a different point of view. This can be useful at times, but not when you're busy trying to sell your company. Bringing in an outsider who has to start from the ground floor might take more time than you have.

There's one other thing you need to be aware of. Everyone on your team who is receiving a fee or is affected in any other way by the sale of your company has at least a modicum of self-interest at stake. It's human nature for a team member to imagine everything from instant wealth to unemployment, and he can act irrationally, at least from your point of view. Without falling into undue cynicism, keep this built-in bias in mind when you make decisions based on the advice you receive. Remember that you are the one who will have to live with the decisions, so make them with your eyes open.

Do You Need a Representative?

Many business owners who are thinking of selling their companies wrestle with whether to hire an agent or adviser—commonly called an "M&A (mergers and acquisitions) specialist"—to represent them in the negotiations. If you decide to hire one of these gunslingers, don't be misled into thinking you can hand everything over to him and hide behind the piano. You need to stay in the saloon and keep your other team members involved. The agent is part of your posse, not a lone gunman.

If you've decided you need an agent, don't wait; get one going now. You can find mergers and acquisitions specialists in most large financial institutions. Since they are in similar fields, ask your financial adviser for a referral, either inside or outside her company. If you feel your business is too small for a large-firm agent, contact a local accounting, law, or investment firm you're comfortable with and ask for a representative or a recommendation.

Steer away from anyone who wants big money up front with no contingency fee. Your representative needs an incentive to get the best price for you. That's the only way to guarantee that his effort will be directed toward closing the deal, not just pencil-whipping the paperwork. A good agent will charge nothing up front and expect to make money on commissions. The best will pay for themselves—they'll sell your business for more than you could on your own.

Here are some of the advantages of having an agent represent you in selling your company.

- **Bottom line.** Because of their experience and access to information, good representatives can negotiate a higher sell price than you could on your own—and more than cover their commissions.
- **Leadership.** If you've never sold a company before, an experienced agent can guide you and your team through the process as a mentor of sorts.
- **Reconnaissance.** The better representatives have access to valuable information about your prospective buyers, including details about recent company acquisitions.
- **Valuation.** A good representative can estimate and present a strong case for the fair market value of your company, based not only on your financial status, but also on an analysis of comparable acquisitions in your industry and the tangible and intangible benefits the buyer will receive from your company, such as increased sales potential of buyer's product, a strong management team, and access to new clients.
- **Time.** While you're busy running your company, your agent, who knows the ropes of selling businesses better than you, can turn a better deal in a shorter time.

- **Objectivity.** A neutral third party is better equipped than you are to purge the decision making of emotions and subjective impressions.
- **Relationship.** If you plan to work for your buyer after the sale, using an agent as a buffer can help defuse any animosity that lingers from tense negotiations.
- **Important trivialities.** A third party helps you address many smaller issues that you might feel are important, such as travel allowances and per diem if you're remaining with the business, but would feel uncomfortable bringing up yourself because you don't want to come across as greedy or petty.
- **Documentation.** A representative can take the lead in producing the offering memorandum (an overview of your company) and financial reports requested by the buyer. Although you'll provide much of the content, your representative can manage the project and package the materials.

A good agent will charge nothing up front and expect to make money on commissions. The best will pay for themselves—they'll sell your business for more than you could on your own.

There are also disadvantages in using an agent or financial representative:

- **Quality control.** Many people claim to be financial representatives; few can back the claim with results. Make sure you hire an agent with a track record of success, preferably one recommended by a trusted source. Get referrals and call them. Be diligent in your selection. A bad choice can prove disastrous.
- **Risk.** Using an agent means putting all your eggs in one basket. Vesting so much power in one person is always risky.
- **Mixed motives.** Your goals and your representative's may differ—you want a home run, he'll settle for a double; he's after the best price (to beef up his commission, of course), you want the best price, plus guarantees for your employees and other considerations. You'll have to be vigilant, monitoring your agent's style and making sure he's working for the results you want.
- **Cost.** Although good agents usually pay for themselves, many financial sand traps lurk in these relationships. Remember that all terms are negotiable. Ideally, the representative will earn all or most of his money on contingency—if and when there's a sale. You'll have to scrutinize all possible expenses, including up-front costs and minimum fees. Nail down exactly what services

he promises. You don't want questions about your agent's role and payment to come up once negotiations begin with your prospective buyers, because at that point the agent will have all the leverage. Get the details in writing and show it to your attorney before you start.

Team Communication

Once you've appointed and launched your selling team, you need to set up a communication plan that will make it easy for all team members to confer with one another and with you in a timely manner. Here are some practical tools to make this happen:

- **Code names.** Regardless of the size of the deal, create a name for the selling project and another code name for each prospective buyer you are negotiating with. Always refer to buyers and the sale process by these code names. This not only helps keep sensitive information from becoming water-cooler gossip, it goes far in making team members feel more a part of something big.
- **Team contact list.** Draw up and distribute a list of team members' contact information. Worksheet 2B at the end of this chapter will serve as a template. You can choose whom to give the list to and whom to keep out of the fray.
- **Regular meetings.** Schedule regular daily or weekly conference calls or online meetings with the entire team. This gives all team members a forum for conferring with others on the team when issues arise, and above all it's a good way for you to quarterback the deal. Each member knows he must be prepared to answer questions from you and the other team members. You'll probably find it's best to hold meetings daily during peak activity, slacking off to every other day or even once a week as the questions get answered and the deal progresses.
- **Task response sheet.** If you have a large number of requests from the buyer, create an online task response sheet that outlines them and assigns responsibility to individuals to respond.

Preparing yourself and your company for the sale is critical for a successful outcome, but it's only half the battle. The other half is to understand the strategies and details of the deal.

WORKSHEET 2A

Putting Together Your Dream Team

Identify individuals who can provide expertise in the following disciplines. List them in order of preference, your top choice first in each category. (It's okay to assign people to more than one role, if they can handle the load.)

MENTOR (GENERAL ADVICE)

NAME:

WORK PHONE: MOBILE PHONE:

FAX: E-MAIL:

NAME:

WORK PHONE: MOBILE PHONE:

FAX: E-MAIL:

NAME:

WORK PHONE: MOBILE PHONE:

FAX: E-MAIL:

ACCOUNTANT (FOR COMPANY)

NAME:

WORK PHONE: MOBILE PHONE:

FAX: E-MAIL:

NAME:

WORK PHONE: MOBILE PHONE:

FAX: E-MAIL:

NAME:

WORK PHONE: MOBILE PHONE:

FAX: E-MAIL:

ATTORNEY

NAME:

WORK PHONE: MOBILE PHONE:

FAX: E-MAIL:

WORKSHEET 2A

Putting Together Your Dream Team (Cont.)

NAME:

WORK PHONE: MOBILE PHONE:

FAX: E-MAIL:

NAME:

WORK PHONE: MOBILE PHONE:

FAX: E-MAIL:

REPRESENTATIVE OR AGENT

NAME:

WORK PHONE: MOBILE PHONE:

FAX: E-MAIL:

NAME:

WORK PHONE: MOBILE PHONE:

FAX: E-MAIL:

NAME:

WORK PHONE: MOBILE PHONE:

FAX: E-MAIL:

OTHER (INDUSTRY SPECIFIC)

NAME:

WORK PHONE: MOBILE PHONE:

FAX: E-MAIL:

NAME:

WORK PHONE: MOBILE PHONE:

FAX: E-MAIL:

NAME:

WORK PHONE: MOBILE PHONE:

FAX: E-MAIL:

WORKSHEET 2A

Putting Together Your Dream Team (Cont.)

ACCOUNTANT (PERSONAL)

NAME: ______

WORK PHONE: ______ MOBILE PHONE: ______

FAX: ______ E-MAIL: ______

NAME: ______

WORK PHONE: ______ MOBILE PHONE: ______

FAX: ______ E-MAIL: ______

FINANCIAL PLANNER

NAME: ______

WORK PHONE: ______ MOBILE PHONE: ______

FAX: ______ E-MAIL: ______

NAME: ______

WORK PHONE: ______ MOBILE PHONE: ______

FAX: ______ E-MAIL: ______

TAX AND ESTATE ADVISER

NAME: ______

WORK PHONE: ______ MOBILE PHONE: ______

FAX: ______ E-MAIL: ______

NAME: ______

WORK PHONE: ______ MOBILE PHONE: ______

FAX: ______ E-MAIL: ______

WORKSHEET 2B

The Dream Team Roster

(Distribute this contact information to selected team members as appropriate.)

PROJECT ______________________

GENERAL ADVICE

NAME: ______________________

WORK PHONE: __________ MOBILE PHONE: __________

FAX: __________ E-MAIL: __________

NAME: ______________________

WORK PHONE: __________ MOBILE PHONE: __________

FAX: __________ E-MAIL: __________

ACCOUNTANT (FOR COMPANY)

NAME: ______________________

WORK PHONE: __________ MOBILE PHONE: __________

FAX: __________ E-MAIL: __________

REPRESENTATIVE OR AGENT

NAME: ______________________

WORK PHONE: __________ MOBILE PHONE: __________

FAX: __________ E-MAIL: __________

ACCOUNTANT (PERSONAL)

NAME: ______________________

WORK PHONE: __________ MOBILE PHONE: __________

FAX: __________ E-MAIL: __________

TAX AND ESTATE ADVISER

NAME: ______________________

WORK PHONE: __________ MOBILE PHONE: __________

FAX: __________ E-MAIL: __________

WORKSHEET 2B

The Dream Team Roster (Cont.)

FINANCIAL PLANNING

NAME: ____

WORK PHONE: ____ MOBILE PHONE: ____

FAX: ____ E-MAIL: ____

OTHER ____

NAME: ____

WORK PHONE: ____ MOBILE PHONE: ____

FAX: ____ E-MAIL: ____

OTHER ____

NAME: ____

WORK PHONE: ____ MOBILE PHONE: ____

FAX: ____ E-MAIL: ____

OTHER ____

NAME: ____

WORK PHONE: ____ MOBILE PHONE: ____

FAX: ____ E-MAIL: ____

CHAPTER 3

Prepare Your Company

HAVE YOU EVER SOLD A HOUSE? If you have, or if you've ever gone to some other seller's open house, you'll know that the first thing you do is get your home in the best shape it's been in since the day you moved in. You spend time and money cleaning carpets, making the windows invisible, hosing out the garage, tossing old magazines, getting the paperwork in order, and making the whole house look and smell great. Everything must gleam when the prospects walk through the door—otherwise, that first impression could be the beginning of the end.

Selling your business is a lot like that. The main difference is that a lot more of the sparkle the prospect is looking for comes through in the way your business runs and how you as the leader have set it up. Sure, it's important that the brick-and-mortar side of the business looks good to the would-be buyer when she takes a walk-through tour: Are the phones being answered promptly, do the trucks come and go smoothly, does the operation look professional, are your people happy, is there good energy radiating from the place? But the most important part of the story is in the numbers. Does the business make money? Is it growing? Is the customer base secure? Are there processes in place that make the business run effectively and consistently? These are the questions you answer in your business overview, the way you present your company to the prospect in person and on paper.

It doesn't matter whether your company is huge or tiny, whether it's a one-person home business or a brawny multinational powerhouse, the same rules apply—nothing turns off a prospective buyer faster than a bad first impression. The prospect's first impression of your company, outside of what he has learned about it from a distance, comes from the detailed description of its functions and finances that you present in your overview—including having key processes for performing specific tasks mapped out in written or graphic form. This is very important; it goes a long way in demonstrating that your business is solid, sustainable, and professional. How do I know this? As I've said, I've owned and sold both large and small.

The business overview document is the single most important marketing tool you can have.

Few things repel a prospective buyer more quickly than seeing an exciting acquisition opportunity turn into a lead turkey because up close it looked like a lemonade stand under the management of the Three Stooges. What do I think when I see vague financials, unwritten growth plans, undefined organizational goals and responsibilities, undocumented operational processes, a shape-shifting business model, an unknown customer base, unhinged compensation plans? I think I'm looking at a lemonade stand, and if I'm still even interested, I automatically offer 30 to 40 percent less than I might otherwise. That's how important it is. I know right away that if I were to buy it, I'd have to invest the time to develop the processes that should already be in place.

Now, the business itself may actually be making money and a real value—but there's a huge difference between *being* ready to sell and *looking* ready to sell. If you can't communicate the true worth of your company to your prospect, you're knocking the props out from under your own valuation. The way you present your company to the world will be a huge negotiating edge if you do it right. You don't need to spend much money on this, because the quality comes from the content of what's presented and not necessarily how it's presented. (There's great software out there to make all kinds of pretty graphs and presentations signifying nothing.) With a great presentation and a professional-quality overview, you'll tell the prospect things that will get him pumped about your business and its potential. Then, instead of taking the Three Stooges Special Write-Down of 30 to 40 percent, you'll be on your way to getting that Premium Price.

Even if you're only beginning to think about selling your company, start preparing *now*. Depending on the shape of your business, it can take as long as two years to get ready. If you have that much time to prepare, great. Sometimes, however, an offer comes in before you're ready, and you have to cram a year of prep time into a few weeks. I've been there; it meant working twenty-hour days for several weeks to get the business presentable—but it was worth it. Don't get caught in this situation. It's unnecessary, and it's risky for your current business, because you'll be pulled away from it during your cram session.

Getting It Together

There's a tendency to rush when you're getting ready to sell. Stop. Slow down. You may have only one chance with a potential buyer. Here is a rundown of what you need to do to present the best possible case for buying your company.

Present a bird's-eye view. Regardless of your company's size, the prospect will want to learn about your business, either as part of the offering memorandum or separately. Once the potential buyer is qualified—that is, you know he's serious and has the bucks to buy your business if he decides to proceed—you, too, should want your business overview in his hands. The information provided should be useful when you put together your rationale demonstrating why your company is so wonderful and worth a high sell price.

Design your overview to grab and hold your prospect's attention. Today's audiences are accustomed to an image-based approach, so use graphics liberally. Pie charts, bar charts, flow charts, Gantt charts, Pareto charts, Venn diagrams, tables, exploded views, and other visual tools are best for conveying the essential information about your company vividly and succinctly. Keep text passages short and break them up with bullet points and numbered lists. Take advantage of today's high-tech media for your presentations. For some of my companies, I've created DVDs that accent the uniqueness and efficiencies of processes. They work well, and they're easy and inexpensive to make. Whether you use a computer-generated presentation or some other format, deploy all your resources to highlight your business's features and successes.

Send over only enough material to whet a buyer's appetite. Then arrange to meet with him in person.

Whenever you can, present the overview in person rather than simply sending the material. If the buyer wishes to see some material before meeting with you, I send only enough to whet his appetite—typically, the financials and growth projections. If he asks for more, I ask for an in-person presentation at his offices or a neutral site. I then control the show by my selection of material presented. Setting the meeting also demonstrates his willingness to invest some of his own time in the opportunity, which is, after all, what my other interested prospects are doing—right?

Below is a sample format for a business overview outline that you can adapt to your needs. I use PowerPoint or Keynote presentation software and a projector, coupled with printouts in books as leave-behinds and support documents keyed by page number to my presentation. Present every positive bit of relevant data you can find; if some of the information isn't positive, don't feel the need to share it unless it's specifically asked for or vital to the success of the business.

There's another upside to compiling all this material in the form of a business overview: Even if no sale occurs, addressing each point in detail dramatically increases your understanding and control of your business.

Business Overview Outline

The following items should be included in your business overview presentation or memorandum unless they are not applicable to your specific industry. See Worksheet 3A at the end of the chapter for a more detailed outline that you can use as a template. Several pages from a sample presentation are included in this chapter; the entire presentation can be downloaded at no cost from the book's website, *www.stevekaplanlive.com* in the "free stuff" section.

1. Business Overview
2. Description of Services
3. Clients
4. Operations
5. Information Systems
6. Management and Employees
7. Financial Performance
8. Strategic Vision for Combined Companies
9. Summary

Shore up your accounting. Nothing scares off prospective buyers quicker than shoddy books. Even if you're a small company and you're selling to another small company, consider having some type of audit performed by an outside accounting firm. If you're considering selling to a large company, you might decide to use a national or regional public accounting firm to perform an audit, since, prior to an acquisition, many large companies require board or shareholder approval and audited financials from the businesses they acquire. Notwithstanding recent scandals surrounding

Charting Your Course

Buyers will appreciate simple and clear visuals that portray your business in a professional light. And since so much of the sell process is often in dry, corporate language, grab every chance you can to present your business visually, using straightforward charts and graphs.

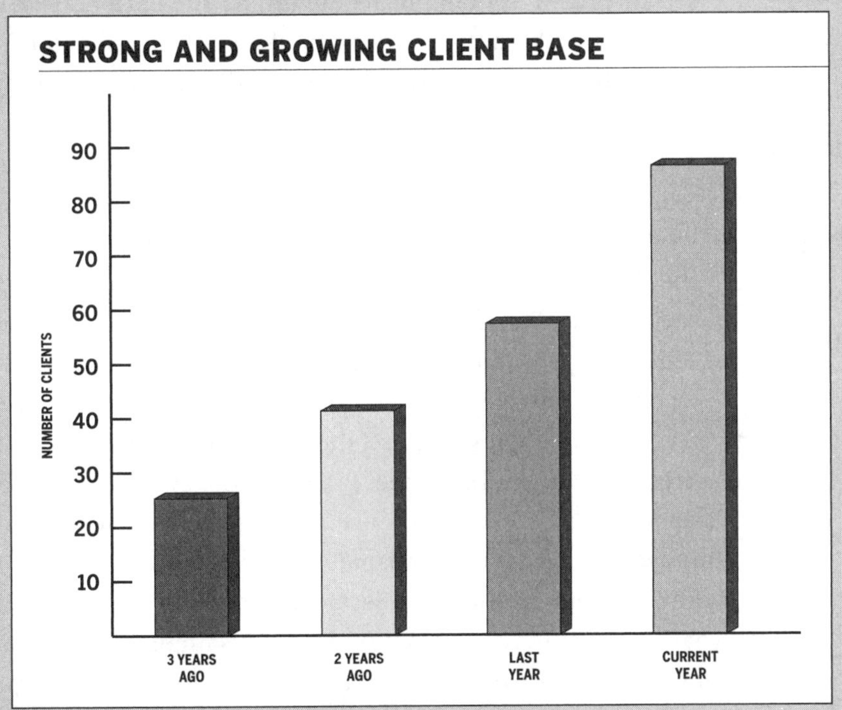

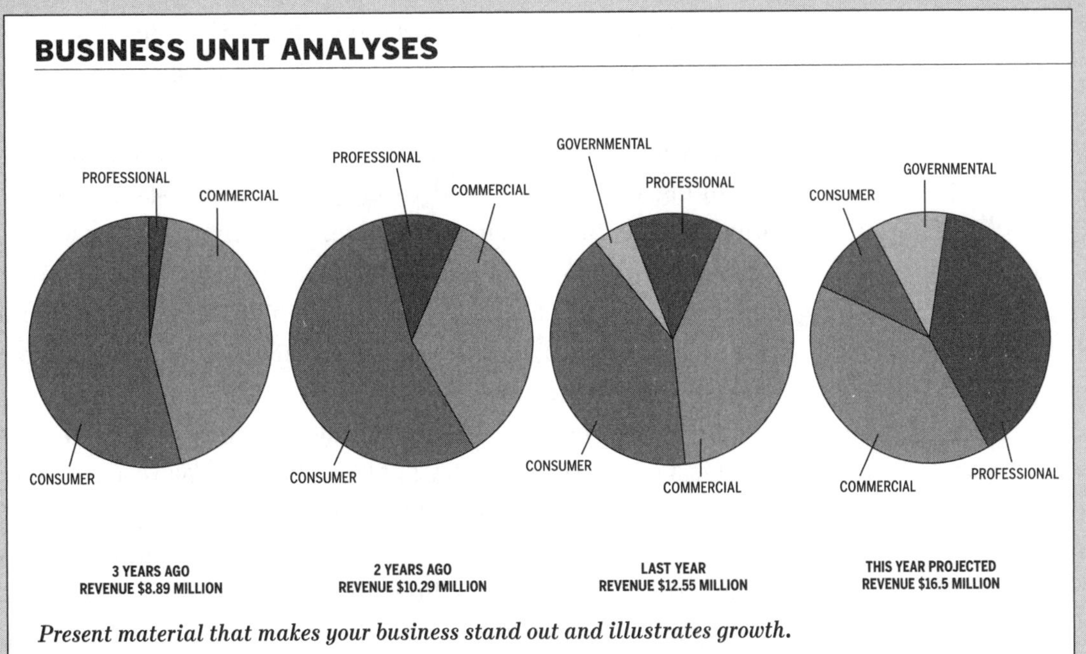

Present material that makes your business stand out and illustrates growth.

some public accounting firms, having your books blessed by one that's still respected goes a long way toward easing the concerns of shareholders and board members. The cost of an audit will vary according to the complexity of your business. Audits can be expensive, so make sure to get several quotes before selecting the firm, and interview regional firms as well as the national ones. If you can't afford the services of a bigger firm, an audit from a smaller firm is better than no audit. In most cases you can get away with a minimum of activity; all you're looking for is the firm's name and the word *audited* on the financial statements to put the buyer's mind at ease.

If your prospect is a competitor, you'll want to make sure you're a little farther down the road before you share your proprietary processes.

Once diligence begins, your accountant will probably be flooded with requests from prospective buyers who may ask to see client lists, financial schedules, payroll and benefits analyses, and much more. Figure out an efficient way to respond to such requests ahead of time. Consider creating several copies of these statements (and those indicated in chapter 8, "Do Due Diligence") in advance, even if you have to hire temporary workers. If you use an outside firm, see if one of its employees can spend more time at your company. At the very least, revisit your business projections for the current and next two years to be sure they are up to date, plus financial statements and balance sheets from the past three years; they will surely be requested.

Show your company's work flow. Define the official procedures for the various operations in your business. If you sell products to customers at retail, for example, prepare a sheet outlining how you select your inventory. If you ship to customers, put together a sheet outlining the process used to keep shipping costs low and your quality control as high as possible. Anything that shows you've thought through every aspect of your business helps instill confidence in prospective buyers. (See chapter 10, "Get the Premium Price," for more on identifying and creating value through process design and branding.)

It goes without saying—but I'll say it anyway—that if your prospect is a competitor, you'll want to make sure you're a little farther down the road before you share your proprietary processes. The prospect will understand your concern here, but make sure to let him know that you have solid work flow processes and are looking forward to sharing them when the time is right. If the prospect isn't a direct competitor, sharing them up front will help you put your best foot forward.

Implement employee agreements. Make sure management and other key people sign employment agreements with non-compete clauses. These documents outline their roles and responsibilities, including compensation packages, termination protocols, and more. A non-compete clause protects the company by prohibiting an employee from working for a competitor after she leaves your company. Having key employees under employment agreements gives the buyer some comfort that the people most important to the business are more likely to stay after the sale, or at least won't work against the buyer. A typical non-compete agreement runs twelve or eighteen months, spells out which activities are prohibited, and lists incentives for compliance. Employment agreements are difficult to enforce if longer than eighteen months; they should be tightly defined in terms of non-compete or other prohibited activities. Check with your attorney on this.

Make yourself dispensable. It's risky for one company to purchase another when the owner of the selling company appears to be a one-person show. Since you're being judged and rewarded on your ability not only to build and sustain an organization, but also to turn it over to the buyer in great shape, don't be afraid to delegate more responsibility than you might be inclined to. Resist the urge to pump yourself up too much; you'll get more mileage if you pump up your managers instead. The best thing a buyer can hear is that the company could run itself if you disappeared—an impression even more important to convey if you want to leave or to move up to another position in your buyer's company.

When I sold my first company, it took me three years to extricate myself. In the meantime, I lost out on many wonderful personal opportunities because I was stuck in a company that wasn't ready to stand on its own. The experience taught me one of my first lessons: Surround yourself with a solid team and make them perform. This is such an important issue that I've devoted all of chapter 13 to making yourself expendable by building an organization and a proper succession plan.

The best thing a buyer can hear is that the company could run itself if you disappeared.

Create a succession plan. Prepare a written plan for the unlikely possibility that you or key employees are stricken by an illness or other tragedy. A well-constructed, visionary plan will show the buyer you're a realist, capable of thinking of the business beyond your own role.

Refine your business model. Create a projected profit-and-loss statement for the next three to five years. Include specific goals and tactics and the procedures needed to realize them.

Illustrate your organization. Create a detailed organization chart, complete with names and titles.

Clear client debts. Collect as much as possible of the money owed you. Buyers are often concerned if it takes a company too long to get paid or if receivables are uncomfortably large.

Cut client dependency. Avoid giving the impression that you're overly dependent on one or two clients. Even if you are, you can take the following steps to alleviate the concern that your business would collapse if one of your clients left:

- Show that you have long-term contracts.
- Show that you have contracts from a variety of different budgets, departments, or offices within the client company that aren't dependent on one another.
- Show glowing client evaluations or any other evidence that demonstrates how committed your clients are to your company, including how deep you are into that customer's organization—that is, relationships at various levels. You might even include your method for growing that relationship.
- Before closing, talk to your top clients and ask them to assure the buyer that the account is solid. Let clients know ahead of time why you're selling the company, and emphasize how the change will benefit them.

Share the wealth. Put your best foot forward by sharing the customer profile you've put together. For security's sake, only show the *type* of information or data you have on your customers—not the information itself. This not only demonstrates that you understand your clients, it also whets the buyer's appetite for the data and any additional value it might hold.

Zip that lip. Guarding your trade secrets is always a good idea, especially when negotiating a sale; it cultivates an air of mystery about your hidden assets, and it protects your company in case the deal falls through. When possible, defer responding to requests for such information until late in the process, and be only as forthcoming as necessary to bring the prospect along. For example, if a buyer inquires about your customer database, limit your answer to a list of the types of data you have or to a one-page printout with a few sample records.

Stamp "Confidential" on any document or letter you send to the prospective buyer or its agents. Before you engage in detailed discussions, have the prospect sign a nondisclosure agreement, which requires, among other things, that all parties keep the discussions confidential, return any documents and copies if the deal falls through, and refrain from poaching each other's employees. Any corporate attorney can provide you with a template, so have the agreement prepared ahead of time.

Gather value and equity. Create a document illustrating your company's value. Include, as discussed in chapter 10, every brand you've developed and its USP (unique selling proposition)—the tangible or intangible quality that makes your product or service rise above its competition. Inventory your information technology assets, including hardware and software, and prepare a document that explains how you use any state-of-the-art technology.

Merge and conquer. If you have business partners, it's time to put aside any disagreements or resentments and come together as a team. One of you can focus on the sale of the business while the others continue running the business. This delineation makes sense not only for you, but also for the buyer, who nearly always prefers negotiating with just one person from the seller's company. If you're the one representing the group, be sure to keep your partners up to speed.

WORKSHEET 3A

Business Overview Outline

The following items should be included in your business overview presentation or memorandum unless they are not applicable to your specific industry.

1. BUSINESS OVERVIEW

Company History
Summary of Products and Services
Business Strategy
Core Competencies: What You Do Best
Selected Investment Considerations: What You Want the Buyer to Know
(Include some simple financial and growth data here, along with any other items that cast you in a highly favorable light.)

2. DESCRIPTION OF SERVICES

Detailed Overview of Products and Services
Business Units: Your Different Divisions, Plants, etc.
Benefits to Clients
Growth Strategy
New Initiatives/Businesses

3. CLIENTS

Chart: Number of Clients Past Five Years
List of Clients
Chart: Repeat Customers
Customer Retention Strategy: How You Keep Your Customers
Client Case Studies

4. OPERATIONS

Operations Flow Chart, Logistics: How You Operate Your Company
Overview of Operations
Breakdown of Operations Components by Department
Invoicing and Billing Procedures

5. INFORMATION SYSTEMS

Overview
Database
Expansion

WORKSHEET 3A

Business Overview Outline (Cont.)

6. MANAGEMENT AND EMPLOYEES

Management Organization Chart (by Position, Not Name)
Department Organization Chart (by Position, Not Name)
Management Compensation Philosophy: Salary Plus Incentive Bonus, etc.

7. FINANCIAL PERFORMANCE

Overview
Chart: Past Three Years Plus Upcoming Year's Estimate
Charts: Revenues, Gross Margin, EBITDA, Operating Income

8. STRATEGIC VISION FOR COMBINED COMPANIES

9. SUMMARY

Key Points for Buyer to Take Away

CHAPTER 4

Identify Prospects

THE DECISION TO TRY TO SELL YOUR COMPANY usually comes in one of two ways: (1) You were approached by another company or person who has made or is considering making you an offer, or (2) the idea occurred to you even though nobody has yet shown an interest in buying you out. In the second case, you need to figure out which companies would be best to approach with a sale offer; in the first case, unless you are ready to accept the first offer outright, you need to identify other potential buyers. The more interest you can stir up, the better your chances of starting a bidding war—and reaping the reward that you've earned from all the sweat, tears, and perhaps blood that you've invested.

So, what does a buyer look like? To answer this question, let's look at it from the perspective of a company that might be interested in acquiring yours. What reasons could the prospect have for buying you? What business purpose would it serve? What does the buyer stand to gain? How would owning your company help the prospect's bottom line? In short, what kind of company would buy You, Inc.?

There are, as you would expect, many possible answers, more than we could possibly list. But we can make it easier by classifying your potential buyers in five broad categories:

- Direct competitor buyers
- Complementary service buyers
- Financial buyers
- Preservation buyers
- Opportunity buyers

We'll look at these different kinds of buyers in detail and show how to identify particular companies that might want to buy yours. First, read the chapter straight through; then go back to the beginning and read it again, this time using Worksheet 4A at the end of the chapter to identify potential buyers. Take time to research each type of buyer profiled below.

Direct competitor buyers. This is one category you already know; these are the guys you're fighting every day for the customer's dollar. Though it's always risky opening the prospect of a sale to a competitor, these are the businesses that obviously understand your industry and your place in it, because they live in that world as well.

Complementary service buyers. Ask yourself: Whom can I help, and how can I help them? Complementary buyers are those businesses that would acquire you because you would help their existing business to grow.

Here is what complementary buyers might want:

- **You have customers they want but can't seem to get.**
- **You have a distribution channel that would help their business.**
- **You have production capabilities they can use.**
- **You have inventory, warehouse, or office space they need.**
- **You have operational expertise that can help them increase profitability.**
- **You have a patent for a technology they can leverage.**
- **Your services add to a more complete vertical offering.**
- **You have personnel resources they can use.**

Spend time identifying these potential buyers; there should be many. Analyze all your areas of operational expertise, the things that make you unique, your processes and ways of doing things, and your competitive advantages. Ask yourself who might benefit from these things and write them on your worksheet.

Financial buyers. Financial buyers—holding companies, private equity fund managers, venture capital groups, and the like—are the ones most often overlooked when identifying prospects. They aren't necessarily focused on your industry, so you may not encounter them regularly or even know their names. Their business is acquiring smaller businesses to either integrate them with other businesses they own, keep them running autonomously with some help to build profits, break them up and sell or absorb their assets, or "flip" them—build them up and sell for a profit.

Even if you have a small business, the right financial buyer might be the perfect fit.

Financial buyers have objectives and mandates that they follow, which makes it pretty easy to tell if they're right for you. For example, rather than a publicly traded company that buys businesses with sales of $5 million to $20 million, you might be a better fit for one focusing on the specialty food business and acquiring companies with sales of $200,000 to $1 million.

Holding companies are usually large entities; many are publicly traded. They specialize in acquiring businesses that, along with profits, will bring them increased capability, better customers, more vertical integration, or expansion into new geographies. I spent years working for a holding company, acquiring businesses that fit into our model—strong growth potential, solid management teams—and that enhanced our bottom line. Other mandates were to stretch the space we competed in so we could offer a more complete, vertically integrated range of products and services to our clients. We also looked for businesses in another geographic market—Europe, for example—or in an untapped domestic market.

Even though your business would, in most cases, maintain its own profit-and-loss records after being bought, holding companies basically like to roll up company financials into one set of master financials that they report to the financial markets (the "street"). Depending on the economic climate, accounting rules, and other factors, they often have the flexibility to pay you a little more than other buyers and are also inclined to snatch you away from competing holding companies. As prospective buyers, it's hard to top holding companies; you should seek them out vigorously.

Private equity funds are institutional products with a business model similar to holding companies, with two major differences: (1) They might be owned by a group that sells large positions to institutional entities, such as Goldman Sachs and Deutsche Bank, who then resell a portion to their high-net-worth individual clients; (2) they buy businesses for the sole purpose of selling them when the time is right according to their mandate.

WHO'S BUYING?

There are many potential buyers out there. They fit into one of five categories.

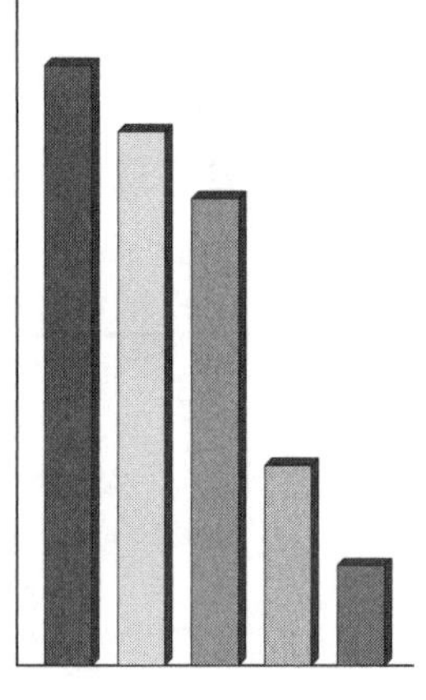

I participate in several private equity funds. This lets me invest in multiple businesses that have been analyzed, meet criteria published by the fund manager, and are under constant scrutiny by the fund manager as well as the financial institution that sold the position to its clients. Having a position across many private businesses spreads your risk, so your return is more stable and predictable. The great news for you is that these funds look for businesses with growth potential so they can sell them later for fancy profits for their investors. Many of these funds are industry focused, and all are predicated on growth, so if you know how to position yourself (and you will, after reading this book), these funds can be an attractive option for you, even if it's just for use as leverage against another potential buyer.

Venture capital groups. VCs range from big-money organizations with hundreds of companies in their portfolio to smaller ones with but a few. They invest in companies, mostly alongside other shareholders, at predetermined stages of company growth, from start-ups to operational businesses to companies getting ready to go public. They may or may not be able to help your company grow. Sometimes VC groups will acquire 100 percent of a company—which is what you want. Usually they follow a buy-and-sell strategy, flipping a business for profit.

Preservation buyers. There are times when one company buys another just to protect its position in the marketplace or to make sure that a competitor doesn't get the upper hand. Such a buyer could even be a current customer of yours, especially if you have worked with it to develop proprietary or custom services. Ask yourself this question: Who will be concerned if Buyer A acquires my business? List these companies on the worksheet; they are potential buyers. Do the same for Buyer B, and so on.

Opportunity buyers. Never overlook the opportunity buyer, the individual looking for a business to get into. There are more experienced potential entrepreneurs out there today than ever. The economy sours, large Company A has a bad year and lays off five hundred people, many of whom are middle and upper management; what do you have? Five hundred people looking for work, some of them looking for businesses to buy. An executive position in big business used to be security, but that's no longer the case, and it hasn't been for quite a while. The only real security is to own your own business and sell it for big dough; then you're secure. Other opportunities come along when companies have a big year and actually make too much money. Often they will seek to reduce their earnings enough to meet or slightly beat earnings projections by investing in future growth. This is where your availability means opportunity for you and the big earner.

Looking Through the Window

When it comes to selling a company, information is golden, and absolutely critical to success. The more you know about potential buyers, their industry, the players, and their motives, the better your chances of closing the big deal.

Consider some of the means I typically use to gather intel on potential buyers for companies I'm trying to sell. You'll be happy, and perhaps a bit surprised, to learn that the best techniques are common sense coupled with a bit of creativity. Some sources will be more effective than others, depending on the category of buyer you're seeking.

Industry associations. Almost every industry has associations that promote it and support the success of its members. Some of the larger industries—manufacturing, retail, marketing, health care, automotive, food and beverage, sales and marketing, government—have multiple associations promoting both the industry in general and particular segments of it. For example, the sales and marketing industry has the American Marketing Association, the Promotion Marketing Association of America, the Direct Marketing Association, the Electronic Retail Association, and many more.

More than 80% of business owners I talk to have no idea where to search for solid acquisition intel.

As soon as you start looking, you'll find plenty of valuable information about your industry. Contact your industry association and read about the services they offer, including details on membership, which might prove worth the cost. As a member, you can check out other association members as potential buyers. Review associations in complementary industries as well.

Industry publications. Browse your trade magazines and online resource guides. Note the companies that are in the news. Who are the newsmakers? What are they doing? Seek out complementary industries and analyze who is doing what. When you find smaller businesses, research them online to see who owns them, then research the owners to see if they are appropriate to engage. Remember to look for the publication's rankings; these lists typically come out annually and often reveal potential buyers galore. Check out the largest companies that are growing, the ones growing fastest, the most innovative—whatever criterion the publication ranks, you'll want to know. A trip to the library or online might just do the trick.

Hit the Stacks

Put on your charm suit and take a trip to the library reference desk. Throw yourself at the mercy of the reference librarian and explain what you're looking for. You'll be pleasantly surprised at just how much he wants to help you and how much he knows about where to dig up great resources.

Online search engines. Technology makes it so easy now it's almost unfair. Go to your favorite search engine and start browsing. Search industries, keywords, complementary industries, companies, recent acquisitions, and more. For example, a Google search for "restaurant industry acquisition" will show a mixture of results, many of which will be recent acquisitions of restaurants and restaurant chains by other companies. Websites of specific companies will usually have information on recent acquisitions, either by them or of them. Search for private equity funds and venture capital groups, then dig into their sites to see if you can find a potential buyer fit.

Supplier network. Although it's not the first thing you might think of, your suppliers can be a unique and valuable source of information. The companies that sell you raw materials, outsourced payroll services, printing, storage—all kinds of products and services—can provide you with great information on other companies they service. I used to get all kinds of great intel from my suppliers, who sold to a few of my competitors and clients as well. Now and then I would ask them what's up over at Company XYZ and they'd fill me in on the latest gossip.

Conventions and trade shows. Look for ads promoting major conventions and trade shows relevant to your industry, and attend them with your eyes and ears open. Once you've learned the names of prospective buyers, visit their websites. Read their growth strategies, learn about their product line, and think of ways your business could enhance their offerings. If they list recent acquisitions, don't hesitate to call a few of the people who have sold companies to them; their perspective can be interesting and instructive.

Financial advisers. Here's another creative way to obtain a ton of great information, one that has worked well for me. Most big financial management institutions deal in banking, equities, fund management, mergers and acquisitions, and other transactions. Most firms have particular areas of expertise in analyzing the marketplace. Collectively, they have enormous data resources on almost every major industry, including tons of material on who in your industry is currently buying, recent acquisitions, formulas used to determine valuation, and much more. They assign people to cover particular companies and specific industries, then develop recommendations on whether to buy, hold, or sell specific company stock. This means these financial experts have enormous amounts of information that can be valuable to you not only in developing your prospect list, but for every step of making the deal.

You're now on the road to becoming a high-net-worth individual, and when you do, you will become a person of interest to these financial institutions. They'll want you to use their services to diversify, manage, and protect your fortune. They'll battle one another to get their hands on your money. So why not take advantage of that competition in advance? You don't have to hire them yet—just indicate an interest in their services and ask them to help you identify companies that might buy your company. Put their experts to work for you now to maximize the amount you will have available for them to manage later. Let them show you how much they can help you and how resourceful they can be. It's a good way to see how these firms work and whether or not they're the ones to handle your fortune post deal.

You'll be amazed at the wealth of knowledge and resources available to you if you just know whom to ask.

Call one of these firms and arrange a meeting with someone who deals with high-net-worth individuals. Explain that you're planning to sell your business and are interested in finding someone to manage the proceeds for you. You can generally count on getting excellent leads from these people.

WORKSHEET 4A

Potential Buyer by Category

Use this worksheet to identify as many potential buyers in each category as possible.

DIRECT COMPETITOR BUYERS

COMPETITOR	BUYER (PARENT COMPANY IF DIFFERENT)

COMPLEMENTARY SERVICE BUYERS

Use the categories below to identify potential complementary valuation in your company.

OPERATIONAL EXPERTISE: LIST YOUR AREAS OF OPERATIONAL EXPERTISE

COMPANY UNIQUENESS: LIST THE THINGS THAT MAKE YOUR COMPANY UNIQUE

PROCESSES: LIST YOUR PROCESSES (WAYS OF DOING THINGS THAT MIGHT BE BENEFICIAL TO OTHER COMPANIES)

COMPETITIVE ADVANTAGES: LIST YOUR COMPETITIVE ADVANTAGES

COMPLEMENTARY SERVICE BUYERS—PROSPECT LIST

Based on the attributes you identified above, write down the name and owner of each company that might benefit from acquiring your business.

	COMPANY	OWNER
Operational Expertise		
Company Uniqueness		
Processes		
Competitive Advantage		

WORKSHEET 4A

Identifying Potential Buyers (Cont.)

FINANCIAL BUYERS

List all potential financial buyers by type

HOLDING COMPANIES:

PRIVATE EQUITY FUNDS:

VENTURE CAPITALISTS:

PRESERVATION BUYERS I

List the potential buyers from the worksheet above in the company column. Answer the following question for each: *If this company buys you, what other companies will be concerned or feel that they are being put at a disadvantage?* Whenever the answer is another company, list that company on the Buyer Prospect list.

COMPANY	BUYER PROSPECT	BUYER PROSPECT	BUYER PROSPECT

PRESERVATION BUYERS II

List the customers you have developed, for which you customized your services, or to which you provide a unique service that they cannot get anywhere else.

COMPANY

OPPORTUNITY BUYERS

List people or contacts that you think might be in the market for a business.

PART TWO

Negotiating the Deal

...

CHAPTER FIVE
Ignite a Bidding War
Page 67

CHAPTER SIX
Negotiate Effectively
Page 73

CHAPTER SEVEN
Payout Structure and Currency
Page 81

CHAPTER EIGHT
Do Due Diligence
Page 91

CHAPTER NINE
Popping the Cork
Page 107

CHAPTER 5

Ignite a Bidding War

SO NOW YOU'RE THINKING SERIOUSLY about selling your business. You're positioning it for the sale, putting out a few tentative feelers, and pulling together a comprehensive overview of your business, including finances, processes, market analysis, client and vendor descriptions, growth strategy, management team profiles, and every other detail of how your business functions and what it will look like in the future. The result, so far, has been a deathly silence.

You're getting nervous. Selling the company would be a huge, life-changing event. Even thinking about it is nerve-wracking. You have serious doubts. Who would be interested in buying? Maybe nobody will want this business of yours. Maybe somebody will buy it but make a mess of it and put your employees out on the street. Maybe you won't get enough to retire and start your own Gates Foundation.

Then the phone rings. Someone is interested! You're surprised, excited, flattered—and even more apprehensive than before. Can you handle it? Can you make the deal go the way you want? Will you come out a winner, or will you walk out shirtless?

You meet the prospective buyer, explain your business, and talk about how the acquisition could help make it bigger and even more profitable. The prospect seems interested, and you get the impression that a deal can be negotiated.

FORMULA FOR SUCCESS:

BUY BUZZ + KNOWLEDGE + SOLID STRATEGY =

BIGGER MONEY FOR YOU

Word gets out. You get another call. Wham! You've got two interested parties. You make another appointment. This meeting, too, goes well. You think, Wow, there might be something to selling this business after all! The years you spent working nights and weekends might be finally paying off in a big way.

Encouraged by your two unsolicited calls, you decide to give it a shot, check out the marketplace, get a feel for what your business might command. You put together an offering memorandum and send it to twelve strategic prospects. Within two weeks, you've heard from five who are interested in talking to you about buying.

What have you done? You've generated "buy buzz"—that happy momentum that builds when more than one party gets interested in buying your company and your valuation gets a bump. In other words, a bidding war, and you're the victor—unless you throw a bucket of cold water on it or declare, "Mission accomplished!" prematurely.

And whether a bidding war is a structured, formal auction run by a third party or just a negotiating strategy that pits potential buyers against each other is irrelevant. The point is that you are in the catbird seat.

The Buyer's Perspective

The buyer's perspective on bidding wars is, as you might imagine, a bit different from the seller's. Whenever I was the prospective buyer of a business, my typical reaction to a seller who pulled the "other interested buyers" ploy on me was to walk—mostly because I tended not to believe it. It's the oldest trick in the book. The skill is to get the bidding war started while maintaining credibility.

That said, there were instances when I believed the "other party" claim. When I knew my competitor's interest in acquiring a business was strong, I would sometimes push my offer a bit higher than I had planned. (Hey, we all get carried away sometimes.) But when it became clear to me that the price was going to be too steep, I wanted to make sure that my competitor used up as much of his acquisition capital as possible. Then I'd have the advantage on the next opportunity.

The winner in this game of one-upmanship? The seller, of course. No matter which of us ended up with his business, the seller would get top price. Note, however, that if the bidding war is not so much to buy your company as to cripple the other bidder, you can end up getting burned. Suppose two companies who happen to be direct competitors keep topping each other's bid until the price gets higher than you ever imagined it could. You have to ask yourself, What does my company have that's worth so much? Do I own the patent on time travel? Am I employing the world's ten top software architects? If not, what you may be witnessing is Company A trying to drive Company B's bid so high that B will spend all its acquisition money on you and give A an easy ride to the next acquisition. And if Company B bails out rather than top the last bid, Company A may have no intention of paying your price. It's important to observe carefully what your prospects are doing and ask yourself whether the bidding is getting unrealistic. Don't get greedy. Strike the best deal that exceeds your expectations, that is structurally sound, that feels right to you intuitively, and lock it up—*before* one of the parties walks.

The skill is to get the bidding war started while maintaining credibility.

Eight Steps to War

Bidding wars sometimes get started on their own, but you'll probably need to take steps to get potential buyers interested. Here are eight actions to start a bidding war:

Draw up your hit list. Generate a list of potential buyers. Start with the prospects you've identified in chapter 4, then add any others who may come to mind.

Select your lead. Start by going after the five best prospects from your hit list. If you can get a buyer engaged in the process, interest may snowball.

Engage the five in discussion. Give the presidents of these companies a call to gauge interest. Once you have one or two willing to discuss the potential acquisition, you're off and running. You'll probably get a lot of interest; many will want to meet just to take a peek under the hood. That's okay at this stage, because you aren't going to tell them much, other than how great your business is and maybe some very top-line financial or growth information. At the meeting you can knock their socks off and get them pumped up. (We'll cover negotiation in the next chapter.)

Select your stalking horse. A "stalking horse" is a prospect, typically the second one you contact, that you use to put pressure on your primary prospect. If your target is a strategic buyer but not the biggest, your best strategy might be to bring your biggest prospect into play as your stalking horse. Consider all types of potential buyers, but be careful; choose your stalking horse wisely.

Don't use one that's so formidable that it scares away your primary. Keep in mind that any prospect can be a buyer; you'd be amazed at how often the stalking horse ends up making the acquisition.

Generate the want. The key to a successful bidding war is getting several buyers to want you at the same time. Your own salespeople can have valuable input into which competitors are enhancing their offerings, which ones are expanding to other markets, and so on. During the course of your meeting with the prospect's reps, ask them how they are planning to grow and where your business might fit into that strategy. Once you get them talking, listen attentively; they will let you know exactly how to sell them.

During the course of your meeting with the prospect's representatives, ask them how they are planning to grow and where your business might fit into that strategy.

The job now is to position your company as fitting into the prospect's growth strategy. For example, if the buyer sells the same specialty items as you and is seeking new locations, your job would be to laud the wonderful nature of your locations. Once you get going, you'll find it pretty easy. If you've done your homework, you should have a good idea of the company's general growth strategy, so even if the prospect is reluctant to share it, you should still know enough to pique the prospect's interest.

No matter what else your prospects say, remember that they are primarily interested in growth—not only the growth that acquiring your company is expected to bring, but the growth that you are planning to achieve within your own part of the business. The more aligned these growth strategies are, the stronger the prospects' belief in your management skills will be and the more they will want to buy you.

Spread the word—judiciously. Getting the word out to strategic buyers is imperative, but the challenge is not letting your employees get wind of it too early. I've found it best to call the president or owner of each company on your hit list and explain that you've been approached by another company (or several) that is interested in acquiring you, but before you pursue that option, you thought you'd give her a call because you think her company might be a better fit with yours. You'll be amazed at the reaction. Most will want to meet with you, and usually they prefer to be discreet about it. Get one to say yes, and you've got your stalking horse.

Use a go-between. Another way to spread the word discreetly is to use a buffer. Find a person who can contact the top executives at all the companies on your hit list—your financial representative, for example—and say he's heard you are considering selling your business and can arrange a meeting if the prospect is interested in buying. When selecting your go-between, ask him about his methods for generating the bidding war. A good representative will have done this before, successfully, and will be able to explain strategy. Beyond that, trust your instincts.

Play all your roles. To lead a successful effort to sell your company, you have to be part businessman, part actor, part CIA operative, and part poker ace. Play your hand close to the vest. Prospects will try to feel you out about who else has approached you. Your ability to finesse this issue is crucial to your success in generating buy buzz. If you can convince several prospects either that they need you or that they need for their competitor *not* to get you, you have a good shot at instigating a bidding war. Show a sincere interest; ask questions about their businesses; let them know you're looking for the best fit. They will understand the financial imperatives that you are concerned with, so you won't need to push too hard on this point. The important thing at this stage is to keep as many players in the game as you can.

Sidestepping the B.S. Factor

As I mentioned earlier, the instinct of most buyers upon being told of another party's interest in your company is to be skeptical. This is why *you must never fabricate interest by another party:* The risk is too great. If there's really no competing buyer and you scare away your primary prospect, you've bluffed yourself out of a potential deal. This leaves you two choices: Let it go, or go to the departed buyer and beg for mercy. No doubt you can come up with some clever excuse for reconsidering his original offer, but you won't be fooling anyone, and the buyer will have all the leverage he needs to give you a haircut on the offer. It's far better to have a real second or third player in the negotiations, even if their hearts aren't really in it.

CHAPTER 6

Negotiate Effectively

HARVEST COFFEE COMPANY, a neighborhood coffeehouse in a bustling suburb of Philadelphia, was approached by a large chain that wanted to acquire it. Founder Suzanne Baker was ready to sell. Not only was she getting tired of the seven-day, sixty-hour weeks, she knew she wouldn't be able to compete against whichever big chain inevitably decided to set up shop near her in this demographically inviting area.

Suzanne had opened her coffeehouse right after her divorce about four years earlier. Her very first business, Harvest was a labor of love, but there were other motivations: She and her kids had grown fond of food and shelter. With these incentives, she had steadily built a solid clientele and a business with an average annual profit of $80,000. Harvest was doing okay by coffeehouse standards, and Suzanne was certainly making ends meet.

When the inevitable happened—Suzanne had seen other neighborhood coffee bars morph into chain cafés—she was excited. But Suzanne had no idea what a big company might pay for her business. She started thinking about what she wanted. In her perfect world, she would sell her business, take away enough money to be able to pay the bills without the pressure and hours of owning the business, and as a result get to spend more time with her daughters.

The solution came to her in a flash: She would ask for three years' profits (approximately $240,000) and a job managing the place for the new owners. Now all she had to do was negotiate with the prospective buyer for this price.

The buyer opened with an offer of 80 percent of average yearly revenues, typical for acquisitions in their industry. In Harvest's case, this amounted to a price of $175,000—more than 35 percent below what Suzanne wanted.

Suzanne wasn't quite sure what to do. She knew that the price offered could be reduced as they proceeded, and this worried her; she really needed that $240,000. Inexperienced and under enormous stress, she countered with an emotional appeal: She pleaded that she really needed the money, as well as the manager's job, to make ends meet.

The buyer, being an unsentimental business juggernaut, sensed an opportunity and applied pressure. Suzanne was informed that the buyer company was planning on moving into the neighborhood, that she should consider the offer, but that the buyer had no more funds to pay for her business.

Suzanne caved in and took the offer. The buyer accepted her terms on the manager position, which provided her with a continuing income.

We can learn a lot from this sale. In my opinion, Suzanne simply gave away the $65,000, and perhaps even more. What could she have done differently?

First, she could have returned the term sheet with a counter valuation formula—say, 3.5 times the average profits over a 3- or 4-year period (leaving room for negotiation down to 3×). This would have changed the playing field by using a valuation method more favorable to Harvest and using the language understood by the acquiring company.

Using the current valuation terms, percent of sales, Harvest would have had to command a valuation higher than 90 percent of annual sales to arrive at the $240,000 price—a multiple that the buyer had never paid before. But changing the formula to a multiple of profit would have taken away that psychological challenge and allowed Harvest to negotiate on better footing. The negotiations would have been on which multiple of profits to pay rather than percentage of sales. This change of the valuation method would have been a form of "rationalizing the emotional," a tactic I described in chapter 1.

Suzanne's other big miscalculation was to let her emotional need blind her to the nature of the manager's job. She viewed it as a benefit to her that she was desperate to keep; in fact, it was a benefit to the buyer, who would be getting a proven employee who knew the business inside out.

Suzanne could have counteroffered with a price based on a multiple of 3.5 times her annual profit, backed up with a "concession": She would stay on as manager for at least three years even though she didn't want to (wink, wink), to "guarantee" continued profitability by keeping her loyal customers coming in. And she would have had a pretty good chance of getting something close to her original valuation.

Pursuing "The One"

I present Suzanne's story, which is real but heavily disguised, to illustrate a few of the subtle financial and psychological complexities of negotiating the sale of a company. In the last chapter, we discussed techniques for getting several prospects interested in buying your company at the same time; in this chapter, we'll concentrate on what goes on between you and your primary prospect when you are negotiating a deal.

In addition to the steps laid out in chapter 5, "Ignite a Bidding War," here are fifteen things you need to do to negotiate a successful sale.

1. **Understand the game.** Selling your business *is* a game, albeit a serious one. Once you start a dialogue with a possible buyer, keep in mind that every action—every discussion, phone call, letter, e-mail, financial disclosure—is part of the negotiation and calls for its own tactics and gamesmanship. Learn to anticipate what's around the next corner; reading this book from cover to cover will open your eyes to a minefield of potential issues and opportunities. Make your actions consistently professional to maintain the message that the buyer is acquiring a professional organization. This applies whether your business is a one-person gourmet cookie company operating from a home or a multinational company with fifteen hundred employees in fifteen countries.

2. **Set your target price.** Compare economic value with comparable and emotional values to get comfortable with the right valuation formula and amount for your business.

3. **Set the playing field.** Once you agree on a valuation formula (most likely proposed by the buyer), make sure you understand it completely; this formula will become the basis for the negotiations. If the buyer is offering to pay 6 times earnings or 2 times receivables or 1.5 times average revenues over the past three years, know that this is what you must negotiate against. However, as was the case with Harvest Coffee, if you know that another formula would be advantageous for you, the time to get it is at the start, before negotiations begin in earnest. If the buyer offers a multiple of average revenues, but you anticipate getting some new customers at high profit margins, push to use a valuation based on profit margins that include projections for next year if they help your cause. Later in the process, the buyer will resist changing the terms of valuation. You might get your way by taking a hard line, but you get only so many do-overs before the buyer decides your company's not worth the hassle. Get agreement up front on which valuation method to use, then stick with it. Try referencing other sales in the industry as rationale for the formula you prefer; if these are not available, you can say that you manage your business by profit (or sales, or whatever) as a rationale for your valuation method.

4. **Go for the range.** Once you get an official written offer (term sheet) from your prospective buyer, seek to make that the bottom of the range. Let's say the buyer offers a figure of six times your earnings. If you agree, your first condition could be that the valuation be based on an average over three years; then choose years in which your earnings were high. If you had a very good year two years back, include that in the mix. Then negotiate the range. With six times as the low end, propose a range of six to nine times earnings, depending on the shape your business is in on the closing date. Now, here's the sweet part of this deal, if you can swing it: Once you read this book and implement the actions recommended—organizing for self-sufficiency, branding your processes, obtaining client commitments, documenting your company's value, demonstrating good financial health, and so forth—your business will be humming along impressively when you're ready to sign the papers, and you'll be able to argue for and justify that nine times multiple.

5. **Don't blink!** No question about it, you want to receive an offer rather than make one. Get the offer in writing, and have the buyer include the formula used to arrive at the offer. Resist the

temptation to answer the question "What's it gonna take?" or "How much do you want?" Instead, simply ask the buyer to put the offer in writing and say you will give it serious consideration.

6. **Compare valuations.** Do your own valuation, then plug your figures into the buyer's valuation formula to see how far apart you really are.

7. **Know your buyer's vulnerabilities.** Understanding the buyer's pressure points can help you get top price. If Prospect A has just lost several key accounts or sales personnel, you can use it as leverage in the bidding process. The buyer's competitor can also be your ally. Ask yourself the same question you did in the chapter on starting a bidding war: "Which company would hurt the prospect company the most by buying us?" This holds true whether the prospect is a financial buyer or a strategic buyer.

8. **Lead with your strong suit.** Recognize and use your natural advantages throughout the negotiation. If your prospect is a public company and you have higher margins, you can probably help it in that arena. Acquiring you will increase its profit margin, and the larger the impact, the more leverage you'll have. This is even more effective if your buyer has had weak earnings reports recently.

9. **Know the playing field.** Understand that the first set of numbers shared between the buyer and seller sets the high and low ends of the valuation range.

10. **Stay on familiar ground.** Negotiate only within the agreed-upon formula.

11. **Bring in extra ammo.** If favorable, use your upside and comparable values as negotiating points to increase the valuation and close the deal.

12. **Put everything in play.** Negotiate not just for money, but for terms, cash versus stock, stock options for your employees, timing, future position, anything of material significance to you. Measure the value of these issues against the major objectives you set for yourself (see chapter 1, "Valuation").

13. **Sell the organization, not the company.** This will come across during the diligence phase and should be emphasized in your initial discussions with the prospect. Buyers love to buy process-defined, organized businesses with good management,

and they hate to buy problems. So if you can get the buyer pumped on your management team and the many processes your organization has, regardless of how big or small your business, you're well on your way to the higher end of the valuation range.

14. **Put yourself in the buyer's shoes.** When you're answering questions in discussions or presenting your business growth plan, consider how you would feel reading the document or sitting across the table listening to you and your people. Do you sound solid and cohesive, or are you all over the place? If you say you have a great plan for growth, but your manager, when asked about the plan later, says she doesn't know anything about it, what does that say to the buyer? Work closely with your team; consider how you look to the prospect, and the message you're sending. This takes a lot of work and coordination, but it's a small price to pay for the huge sell price you're after.

15. **Be the crown jewel.** When negotiating, make sure to communicate to the buyer just how your business will be the exciting growth aspect of the buyer's current business. Be energetic when talking about growth; let the buyer imagine that surge of new energy.

Avoid the Pitfalls

Negotiating is a complex game. Combine the rules of bridge, chess, and poker, and add in all the strategy and tactics and wiles of the master game players, and you get a notion of what it's like to negotiate your way to a successful sale. There are plenty of hidden dangers for the inexperienced. Here are a couple of common errors to avoid:

Being too cute. Negotiations are progressing, and you're happy because things are going your way. You develop some leverage and use it again and again to get your way. You get so carried away with making the deal better and better that you lose sight of your original objective. Suddenly, one day the buyer has had enough and says adios. You've just hogged yourself out of a sale.

Pigs get fat.
Hogs get slaughtered.

To keep yourself from getting seduced by the thrill of winning tactical victories, keep looking at the personal and financial objectives you drew up in the Introduction. This will help you keep your feet on the ground. Are you obsessing over some minor detail? Does the buyer think you're being unreasonable? Revisit your objectives. If you find you've achieved or surpassed almost every one of your priority objectives, consider backing off the accelerator on that issue. Let the buyer win the point. It will pay off in good will and flexibility on other issues.

Remember, today's adversary may be tomorrow's boss.

Building resentment. You and your prospective buyer will be going through the buy-sell experience together. During negotiations there will be ups and downs, times with immense stress and pressure and times filled with peace and happiness. Remember this: If you're planning to stay with the business after the deal is done, you might end up working with, or even for, this person you're butting heads with. You want this person to respect your negotiating position and ability, of course, but the last thing you need is to have your days filled with animosity between you and your boss. Keep your cool at all times; don't make it personal. If you have one, use your financial agent as a buffer; if not, try to deflect some of the negativity to attorneys or others you may hire for the process. Spread the toughness around; don't be the one to take the hard line every time.

On the other hand, if you are leaving the business post sale, feel free to be the bad guy. This way you can take all the hard feelings with you when you leave.

CHAPTER 7

Payout Structure and Currency

BY THE TIME YOU GET TO THIS PHASE of the deal process, you're feeling pretty good. You've ironed out the amount your company is worth to the buyer, and you're ready to consider, or reconsider, how the value of your company will be transmitted to your pocket. It's a heady feeling. You're another step closer to becoming very, very wealthy. Or at least wealthier. But the money isn't yours yet, and the form and schedule of its arrival can make a difference in how rich you get and how fast you get rich. There are two issues to consider: The timetable for payment, and the nature of the compensation.

The last thing you want to do is make a great deal and not get paid. Believe me, I've seen it happen. You put in all those hours and and then factors beyond your control—poor decisions by the buyer, a bad economy, losing key management—severely diminishes the actual money you receive.

Payout Structure

Usually as part of the term sheet offer phase of the sale, but at times after the sell price has been established, you'll negotiate your payout structure. Now, this has nothing to do with the amount you'll be paid or whether the actual payment will consist of cash, stock, cattle, jewelry, or whatever; rather, it's the schedule under which you'll get what is owed you. Generally the payment can come in one of three ways:

- Up-front payment
- Earn-out over time
- Combination of up-front money and earn-out

UP-FRONT PAYMENT

In this scenario the buyer and seller agree on how much the company is worth, then the buyer pays that amount by wiring funds, presenting a certified check, or issuing stock. It's that simple. If the value seems fair, an up-front payment scheme can work well, because it allows you to move on when the timing feels right or according to the agreement you've reached.

ADVANTAGES

- **Security.** It's the bird in the hand. Having money in your pocket is always safer than waiting for payments over time, which may not be forthcoming if unforeseen problems arise.
- **Leverage.** It's "take a hike" money. If you're planning on staying with the company after the purchase, getting your money now will switch the leverage and power from your new employer to you, because the buyer will have less of a hold on you post deal. This means a less stressful work experience for you.
- **Growth.** It's working money. If you get your money up front and invest it wisely, the interest, dividends, and equity growth can increase your wealth even more. For example: If you receive $5 million and invest it at a modest return, that's an additional $200,000 in year 1, and more in year 2 if you make sure the $200,000 earns interest. In this scenario getting your money over a two-year time frame would mean that you'd need to be paid approximately $400,000 more to match what you'd get with the up-front payment. Make sure you're ready to receive the monies so you can avoid possible crippling tax consequences.

DISADVANTAGES

- **Discounted value.** Your business could be worth a lot more later than it is now, particularly if it's poised for exploding sales and profits. But it can also be worth less in the future, and to mitigate that risk, the buyer will try to discount the price you get now.
- **Taxes.** A windfall can impose a hefty tax burden.
- **Motivation hit.** Many of us, including me, perform better when we're a bit hungry. If you're one of those people and you suddenly come into a fortune, your focus and priorities may change, leaving you a little disenchanted. The result can lead to your falling short on important business or personal goals. Closing the deal in the knowledge that you're going to have to wait a while for the money might give you the time necessary to handle your sudden change in financial status.

In more than 80% of the deals I've been part of, the selling company president has not been comfortable with the change of control.

EARN-OUT

The earn-out is a common payment structure in acquisitions; it's my preference whenever I acquire a business. The reasons are simple: It protects the buyer from overpaying for a company, and it virtually ensures that the seller will remain in place, working hard to increase the company's value during the earn-out period or beyond. It's like saying to the seller, "Put your money where your mouth is." A proper earn-out structure lets the seller make more from the sale, assuming the business meets its projections. This aligns the interests of the buyer and the seller: The buyer wants to pay more for a better-growing business, and the seller wants to get more for providing a business that's bigger and better.

With an earn-out, the seller is paid in installments based on a formula, usually a multiple of the company's earnings or sales and some other predetermined factor. After you've read the disadvantages, spend the time to figure ways to mitigate them. I've included some ideas with each.

ADVANTAGES

- **Pot of gold.** The seller should have a bigger potential upside if the purchased company performs well.
- **Solid compromise.** The earn-out mitigates the buyer's risk and thus makes a deal more attractive. Depending on your business, the economy, and your prospective buyer, this might be the only alternative for you, so you might as well embrace it.

- **Free ride.** Under certain situations, remaining involved with the buyer actually helps your company make more money through access to the buyer's client base and other resources; your company's upside value can pay off for you again.
- **Creative opportunity.** There are times where a company that sold in an earn-out structure receives the benefit of the parent company's accounting opportunities, resulting in larger profits and a much bigger payout down the line.
- **Smooth departure.** If you're considering sticking around for a few years anyway, the earn-out can give you a way to disengage gradually so you can prepare yourself emotionally over a few years to leave the business.

DISADVANTAGES

- **Lack of control.** Once you've sold, you may cede control to the new owner over certain operations in your business. Yet because you're being paid based on your performance, you may not want someone else making decisions that can affect your earning potential. One solution is to include language in your purchasing agreement addressing who controls what. Be sure to maintain control over profit and loss of the business, or else at the end of the day you might end up less than thrilled.

In about 8 out of 10 deals in which the owner continues to be active in the business, the earn-out is higher than anticipated.

- **Thumbscrews.** You'll feel pressure to make as big a profit as possible during the earn-out period because every dollar you make will result in a multiple of that dollar in payout. If you're selling your business in hopes of expediting its growth, worrying about every dollar can make you reluctant to invest in growth. The best solution is to acknowledge this dynamic and include details in the buyout agreement to work around a conflict between profits and growth—for instance, by basing your earn-out on profits before growth investments.
- **No team player.** Since you are paid based only on how your former company performs, you will be inclined to resist anything that impedes profits, including your own assimilation into your buyer's culture and company. After all, time spent away from your business could mean a lower payout for you. Again, a clause in the buyout agreement can provide a safety net if your new boss wants to move you upstairs.
- **Defensiveness.** During the earn-out period, you may feel self-

What an Event!

A few years ago, on behalf of the publicly traded company I was working for, I led an acquisition of Right Now Events, an event company located in the Southeast. The company managed the logistics of setting up and executing big events for large packaged-goods companies. They promoted their products through advertising, giveaways, and other promotional activities and were mostly noted for those fun trucks visible around spring break locations that pumped out the loud music and gave away samples of everything from suntan lotion to cans of Red Bull.

My team worked on the acquisition with Debbie Williams, Right Now's president and owner. The business was in great shape, there were many processes in place, the customers seemed to be happy with the company, the financials were solid (posting earnings of approximately $3.5 million per year), and Right Now had been growing by 25 percent annually for the past four years.

Debbie was very bullish on her business, so we agreed on the following structure: $1 million up front on four times the average profits from the business over the next three years. The initial $1 million would be an advance, deductible from the payout amount. If Debbie's projections held true, she stood to make about $20 million.

Around the time the acquisition closed, I moved on to pursue other activities, but I kept in touch with Debbie throughout her earn-out period. What happened to her was, to say the least, amazing. Debbie explained that the parent company that purchased Right Now had been having some difficult times and was not meeting the profit expectations it had stated to the financial community. The company announced that it would be going through a restructuring of assets that would result in a more efficient, streamlined business. It called in the accountants and sought to utilize every legal accounting tactic to boost profits, and it planned on taking a big write-down on many of its assets. Debbie, sensing an opportunity, went to corporate and presented a plan that would significantly boost Right Now's profits. Among other tactics, the plan called for an up-front full expense of most of the equipment, such as trucks and machinery, instead of amortizing them over many years. The change would trigger significantly higher profits over the years to come.

The parent company jumped at the opportunity, and as a result of this accounting strategy, Right Now's profits soared by an additional 50 percent. Debbie was ecstatic. Because she was being paid for her business on an earn-out, this move increased her average annual profit by about $2 million and the payoff amount by an additional $8 million. Over the earn-out period, the parent company ended up paying Debbie $31 million for the business, $12 million more than what they originally would have paid for the same earnings. Such is the wonderment of the public company arena.

One point to remember is that things can go both ways, and one person's opportunity might be another's nightmare—so, heads up.

protective and skeptical about every interaction with the buyer, imagining late into the night how he's undermining your payout. After a while, all this defensiveness can exact a toll. Take the time beforehand to establish a good relationship and mutual trust with the buyer and keep control over profit matters as discussed earlier; if you can't, and if you have the option, you may be better off with an up-front payment.

- **Risk.** By making your payments contingent on your performance, if your company fails, even for reasons outside your control, you could wind up giving it away for a song. Because there's no sure solution to this one, an earn-out payment structure makes it doubly important to thoroughly check out the buyer. (See chapter 8, "Do Due Diligence.")

Be sure not to become so excited about selling your company that you agree to an unfair earn-out deal. Assess your earn-out structure carefully and consider the effects of worst-case scenarios and other contingencies that might affect profitability.

UP-FRONT/EARN-OUT COMBO

As the name implies, this structure consists of money now and money later. Typically, the lion's share of the payout comes during the earn-out. The up-front money is usually a gesture to help retire debt or because the seller simply demands some money now. Depending on the health of your company, try to get a fair share up-front. You never know what might happen over time, even with the best intentions from both parties.

Be sure not to become so excited about selling your company that you agree to an unfair earn-out deal.

A word of advice: When speaking with the buyer about the structure of your deal, don't get so caught up in the details or blinded by the neon dollar signs pulsating on your eyeballs that you forget the big picture—your future. If you're staying with your company after the sale, have you carefully planned how you can work with the buyer to grow your business? Have you envisioned what day-to-day operations might look like a year from now ? Will the new setup suit you and align with all your hopes and dreams?

Currency

Regardless of the payout structure, at some point you will receive compensation for the business you've sold. This can be in the form of either cash or stock. Which is better

Dream Deal

Several years ago, Global Vacations, a large international travel company, sought to buy Adventure Guides, another travel agency that specialized in extreme sporting vacations.

Although Deirdre Barnes, the owner of Adventure Guides, was initially intrigued, she hesitated, because the increased popularity of extreme vacationing promised exceptional growth for her company. That very trend was, of course, why Global was so interested in her company.

GLOBAL VACATIONS—PROJECTIONS

	Previous Year	Current Year	Next Year	Third Year	Fourth Year
Revenues	$78,000	$153,000	$200,000	$350,000	$500,000
EBIT*	$23,400	$53,550	$70,000	$133,000	$190,000

*(Earnings Before Interest and Taxes)

Deirdre looked at her projected profit-and-loss statements for the next few years. Here's how the numbers panned out:

Deirdre knew that if she sold now, she might miss out on a windfall later. On the other hand, she knew that the extreme sports business fluctuated with economic conditions, and that the buyer had a sterling reputation that could help her win even more business. She decided to proceed with the sale, but she wanted a structure that would let her benefit from what she believed to be her business's tremendous growth prospects over the next few years.

Global offered Deirdre an up-front payout of five times the average earnings (EBIT) from the previous year and the current year, which amounted to $192,375. Because it was concerned about Adventure's ability to grow, Global was reluctant to assume the risk that it might fail and so did not want to factor in Deirdre's growth projections.

Deirdre worked with Global to settle on a structure that would satisfy them both. Global would buy Adventure now but agreed to an earn-out over the next three years based on three times the average EBIT for this year, next year, and the following year. Deirdre would remain in charge until the end of the three-year earn-out period. She agreed to the terms because she knew that if Adventure met or exceeded its projections, she would take in $256,550 or more.

The last time I spoke with Deirdre, she seemed delighted with how things turned out. She'd completed the earn-out period and taken home more than $280,000.

for you? Here's how they stack up:

Cash. Money in the bank is usually your best bet. Set up a wire transfer at your financial institution, and you're good to go. Make sure you get professional tax, investment, and estate advice at least three months prior to receiving your funds.

Stock. Stock lets you own a part of your buyer's company. For many buyers it's also cheaper than paying you in cash. If cash reserves are low, this might be the only way your buyer can acquire you. You can often command a higher sell price if you agree to take stock rather than cash. Of course, the stock can decline in value.

Stock used in purchasing companies is often subject to Securities and Exchange Commission (SEC) rules that place restrictions or lockouts on when you can sell your stock; the typical lockout is one year. As well, the buyer will probably want to restrict your ability to sell stock to ensure that you don't sell a huge block of shares at once and possibly depress the stock price. Make sure you fully understand all applicable provisions as well as tax implications arising from the sale of the stock.

Reducing your stock risk. The market can be highly volatile at times and most of us are reluctant to absorb risk even before we even cash out. If you do decide to accept the buyer's stock, consider the following strategies to minimize your risk:

- **True-ups.** Try to include in the purchase agreement a clause that gives you additional shares if the stock price has fallen below a specified level when your lockout period expires. This could help you recoup some of those losses.

- **Eggs in one basket.** I've seen too many horror shows in which otherwise intelligent business owners get greedy or simply drop the ball when faced with making prudent decisions about their stake in the seller's company. Often people hold on to stock for dear life while their fortunes plummet with it. A good test: Ask yourself if you would ever have bought or held as much stock as you now own in the buyer's company. If the answer is no, and it probably is, consider diversifying your holdings.

- **Traitor!** Sellers often worry that if they sell the buyer's stock, it's like saying they don't believe in the buyer's company. First of all, the officers of the buyer's company have probably sold plenty of their own employer's stock themselves. Second, you have to separate your own personal financial strategy, which includes your tolerance for big risks, from your loyalty to your new company.

- **Piggyback rights.** Public companies sometimes sell blocks of shares through a follow-on (or secondary) offering to the investment community. Piggyback rights allow you to participate in this sale. Check with a financial adviser for a full explanation of piggyback rights to determine whether they're something you should consider in your negotiations.
- **The derivatives world.** Derivatives and other financial instruments rely on puts, calls, options, variable forward options, and other strategies to reduce the risk that your value will drop, even if the stock price drops. Depending on your restrictions, derivatives, which are regulated by the SEC, can be used after a holding period often as short as three months. Check with your financial adviser for more information. I've used derivatives many times, and more than once they've saved me when my buyer's stock price tanked.

CHAPTER 8

Do Due Diligence

ABOUT A YEAR AGO, I was thinking about buying a business in the telecommunications e-commerce industry, a sector I strongly believed in and wanted to get into. I was approached by the company's president and chief technology officer, who spent some time walking me through the details of their business and talked about all the amazing opportunities on the horizon. The New York–based company had a great business model, and its executives told me they had a couple of patents providing some category protection, plus contracts with several huge companies to process the e-commerce for their products.

I wondered: Why are they selling? Why not build the business? The reason, I was told, was that there was quite a bit of infighting between founders. A not-unheard-of situation; the owners couldn't get along and wanted to split the bed sheets and go on to other endeavors. Sometimes you can pick up a real bargain in this situation.

So I got together a few of the people I invest with from time to time, and everyone agreed that the sector, coupled with the business model and company positioning, made this an attractive acquisition, one worth considering. I met with the president several more times to get a better handle on the company's financial situation so that, assuming everything made sense, we could tender an offer.

Based on the information from the meetings, we offered four times average EBITDA (earnings before interest, taxes, depreciation, and amortization) for the past two years and two future years. The exact amount of the purchase price would be an earn-out predicated on exactly how the business performed over the next two years, but the current shareholders would have the opportunity to walk away with up to $8 million if the business reached the levels they had projected (see chapter 7, "Payout Structure and Currency," for more on earn-out structure). We also required that the current president remain with the business to ensure a smooth transition and to drive the business to reach its earn-out potential.

We agreed on the valuation and payment terms, so all that was left was to check under the hood. Was the business a solid, viable entity, a house of cards, or something in between? Due diligence would tell us.

The company was pretty small, so diligence wouldn't be that painful an event for either side. We drafted a list of items we were interested in reviewing—among them copies of the patents, financial statements, and customer contracts—and set up meetings with management, including a demonstration of the technology used by the company as its competitive advantage and barrier to entry.

Three of us descended on their New York offices and started to dig. About twenty minutes in, it was "Houston, we have a problem." One of my partners noticed a few minor issues: The patents that were supposedly a great value weren't actually approved yet; the contracts with those huge companies weren't actually signed and had been in the works for about a month (something is always fishy when contracts take more than a week or so to get signed); and the twelve employees were basically working in a structureless organization with no defined roles, objectives, or accountability.

If that wasn't enough, the next issue was. We did our homework and hired an industry expert, who dug into the technology and informed us that it was very close to what many of the big telecommunications companies were using to get into this space, so the business would soon be in a fight with some heavyweights.

Needless to say, we backed away from the deal in a hurry, and all it really cost us was about two weeks' time and a few legal fees—a small price to pay to avoid the disaster that was poised to fall on us.

Nothing Up My Sleeve

This story shows the importance of due diligence for both the buyer and the seller. The buyer, of course, needs the diligence process to feel comfortable with the health of the company it is buying and to verify the details of the potential purchase. The process is also vital to the seller, who should be using due diligence as a tool to make the buyer feel comfortable with the deal. This means that the seller needs to anticipate what will be needed and work to make sure the important issues are covered. In addition, the seller needs to dig into the facts about the buyer's company to reassure himself that the deal is all that it appears to be on the surface.

The last thing you would want to feel as the buyer is that the seller might be hiding something.

Put yourself in the buyer's shoes for a minute. It doesn't know you or the intricacies of your business, yet it's getting ready to give you some big bucks. The last thing you would want to feel as the buyer is that that the seller might be hiding something. In the case of the company I was looking at, the seller's mistake was letting us discover the deficiencies on our own. That was far more damaging to the seller than if the seller had known and disclosed the problems up front. In fact, it made us back away from the purchase in a big hurry.

Remember that the deal isn't done until it's done, and most that fall apart do so in the diligence phase, so you *must* fully understand the process, what your buyers are looking for, and, most important, how you can use due diligence to actually enhance their interest and desire to get the deal done. In effect, you must control the process without appearing to do so. It must appear to be a completely open process, and to a large extent it is, but in reality you are deciding what they see, how they see it, and when they see it. All of these give you a great advantage.

The Diligence Process

Once you've set forth the basics of the proposed deal, it's time to sit down with the buyer and delve into the details of each other's companies in the process known as due diligence. Typically, the buyer will take a long, hard look at your company. As the seller, you also have the right, even the duty, to do some digging into your potential owner.

SELLER'S DUE DILIGENCE LIST

As a business owner, selling your company may be a once-in-a-lifetime opportunity, so you must do your best to make sure the buyer is right for you—that it has the financial strength to make the buyout payments, invest in your company, and facilitate your growth. Seller's due diligence gives you the opportunity to check out your new partner. This is something you should take advantage of, even if you're not particularly inclined to, because it's a solid negotiating tool.

Putting the buyer on the defensive (just a little bit) and requiring it to sell you on the deal creates the perception that you're not fully committed to its being the buyer. Perhaps there are other players, or perhaps you will put off selling your business. Whether this is the case or not, seller's due diligence helps level the playing field.

Often a prospect will ask you to give it exclusivity—that is, entertain no other offers while the two of you try to work out a deal, at least through the buyer's diligence phase. You would prefer to leave the field open, of course, but if the buyer is adamant, exercise your seller's diligence before you agree. Can the prospect make good on its offer? If you are satisfied that it can and you're comfortable selling to it, go ahead and grant exclusivity, but impose a time limit. The period can vary, depending on the size and complexity of the buyout, but sixty days is typical.

As the seller, you need to bring up the following issues for discussion (some may not apply to you) and ask for the relevant documents. Divide the process into stages. Focus initially on how the buyer views your company and its growth in general, rather than on the buyer's financial statements or how much you'll be paid as an employee. Remember that the buyer wants to buy a solid business, and one of the most important aspects of a solid business is leadership. If you're perceived as caring only about the money, you're not likely to get as generous an offer as you would if you showed you're concerned mostly about the growth of your business after the sale, regardless of whether you're going to be there or not. After all, that's precisely what the buyer hopes to achieve by acquiring your company.

BUSINESS INQUIRIES

- How will your company be run and by whom?
- How does your company fit into the buyer's long-term strategy?
- What steps will the buyer take to increase your business?

- Will you need to change the way you handle your accounting?
- What other companies does the buyer own?
- Whom will you report to and how?

EMPLOYEE INQUIRIES

- What will happen to your employees after the sale?
- What benefits are offered to employees?
- Can you issue stock options to your own employees?
- What are the key provisions of the buyer's employee handbook?

FINANCIAL HEALTH INFORMATION

- Financial statements from the past three years
- Balance sheet from the past three years, including cash and receivables. This will show you the prospect's buying strength.
- Client list, including potential conflicts of interest and business opportunities
- Annual report (if the buyer is publicly traded)
- Any pending litigation and the disposition of any lawsuits filed in the past three years
- The buyer's strategy for growing its business over the next three to five years
- Organizational chart and how you fit in

Remember that the buyer wants to buy a solid business, and one of the most important aspects of a solid business is leadership.

BUYER'S DUE DILIGENCE

If you're selling to a smaller company, due diligence can be short and sweet. If, however, you're selling to a larger company or a publicly traded one, it will probably demand a mountain of information because of its fiduciary duty to its shareholders.

The diligence process can lead to one of two results:

1. Validating what you have represented in your discussions

2. Giving the buyer a reason to back out of the deal

To ensure a favorable resolution, you should carefully follow the steps outlined in chapter 3 on preparing your business for a sale, and consider the following strategies as well:

- Ask for the buyer's due diligence list as early as possible and start working on it immediately.
- Be sure not to misrepresent anything or overpromise during discussions or negotiations.
- Before you discuss any details of your business or send anything to a prospective buyer, have the buyer sign a confidentiality

Don't just do due diligence. Overdo it.

agreement. Often referred to as a CA or NDA (nondisclosure agreement), this document will protect the confidentiality of the material you share and the discussions you have with this company, which may or may not buy you. Make sure to include a clause that requires the potential buyer to return all documents, including copies made by them, that were sent at any time during the process. Any business attorney will have a boilerplate CA on file, so the cost to you should be nominal. I've included a copy as Worksheet 8A, but if you use it, have your attorney review it first to be sure it's right for you.

- Go out and buy a "confidential" stamp, then mark every exchanged document as Confidential.
- Present all the information requested neatly and concisely.
- Treat the process as a legal proceeding: Answer the questions asked and nothing more. Remember, you've already made the sale.
- Set up a data room off-site; your attorney's office is a good place. Designate a conference room or large office for the purpose. Make sure all documents are easily accessible. If it has to be in your offices, set the hours that data will be accessible, and be there yourself to explain the documents and answer questions; if necessary, have your attorney be there at all times.
- If the buyer wants to meet your key employees or clients, wait until the final stages of closing the deal; you don't want a loose cannon contradicting anything you've said. Also, keep in mind that if the deal falls through, you may discover that your data room has been a de facto interviewing room and that your ex-buyer has stolen some of your best people. If possible, wait until the deal terms have been negotiated to inform your management and staff of the deal.

Sample Buyer's Due Diligence List

The following is a sample due diligence list. The one I've included is comprehensive, suitable for a large publicly traded company; most transactions rely on shorter versions. If you have no idea what some of these documents are, you're beginning to get the idea of how much homework due diligence can involve. The more you can anticipate and overdeliver on the buyer's needs, the smoother the process will go. You will find a slightly longer version of this list at the end of the chapter. Use it to check off each applicable diligence item once you have compiled it; write "NA" next to items that are not applicable to your business.

1. **Corporate Structure**
   Capitalization table of seller to show equity ownership
   Seller's corporate structure chart
   Management organization chart
   Board of directors information

2. **Corporate Organization Documents**
   Seller's certificate of incorporation with amendments and bylaws
   Minutes of board of directors meetings
   Board of directors and shareholder consents
   Stock ledger

3. **Accountants' and Auditors' Reports and Financial Statements**
   Audited financial statements for each of the past three years
   Consolidated income statements
   Audit response letters from counsel
   Miscellaneous financial information
   Revenue recognition policy
   Pro forma projections over the next four years
   Year-end financial statistics from current year or most recent year

4. **Acquisition Documents**
   Asset acquisitions from past ten years
   Documents related to recapitalization of seller's companies

5. **Contracts**
   Confidentiality agreements between seller and key clients
   Sample purchase order form
   Summaries of contracts
   Operations contracts and related information
   Consulting services agreements
   Accountant's consulting documents
   Equipment leases
   Lease agreements

6. **Debt Arrangements**
   Summary of long-term debt arrangements
   Credit agreements

7. **Employee Information**
   Human resources report
   Chart of employees by region
   Employee summaries (hourly versus salaried)
   Management information
   Management salary information

Management organization charts
Payroll information

8. **Employee Benefits Information**
   Benefit summary
   Benefit plans and related information
   Sample noncompetitive and nondisclosure agreements
   Severance pay agreements
   Stock option plans
   Seller's executive deferred compensation plan
   Employee bonus information
   Employee disability, leave, and vacation information
   Sample option grants
   Flexible benefits plan information (Form 5500, etc.)
   Employee car allowance information
   Schedule of stock option grants
   Profit-sharing retirement plan

9. **Intellectual Property**
   Patent, trademark, and copyright status reports

10. **Insurance**
    Insurance coverage summaries
    Insurance information—loss summaries, etc.

11. **Environment and Safety**
    List of issues
    Environmental reports (past four years)
    Miscellaneous environmental information

12. **Sales Information**
    Sample sales brochures and other information
    Sales-related surveys
    Business overview presentation

13. **Tax Matters**
    Historical tax information
    Tax returns
    Tax provision information (past three years)

14. **Real Property**
    Lease 1 ____________________
    Lease 2 ____________________

15. **Appraisals of relevant property**
    Property 1 ____________________
    Property 2 ____________________

16. Miscellaneous

Information on pricing analysis
Database information
Depreciation expense reports
Press releases
List of top ten clients over the past three years
Locations of inventory
Lease obligations
Incremental capital requests, if any
Competitive chart and summary

The Data Room

Setting up a data room for the prospective buyer is a must; it lets you maintain control of the process and your proprietary information. The data room should be filled with items from the Buyer's List above along with other items that will show the company in a good light—references from clients, magazine articles, a business plan, overview sheets showing client repeat or growth figures, and anything that shows the organization as professional and process-oriented. Include a printout of your business overview; this will reinforce some of the key aspects of your business. If you can't get everything, don't worry; just let the buyer know, and it will tell you whether the item is vital. Typically it's not, unless it's something like financials, which, of course, are absolutely essential.

A good data room will set the scene for a quick, painless diligence process and have a tremendous impact on getting you the deal you want.

Organize the data room so the items are easy to find. Number the items to correspond with the numbers on the diligence list. This is the accepted method, and it will demonstrate your professionalism. Before the buyer arrives, take one final lap through the data room; make sure there's nothing there that doesn't belong or that you don't want anyone to see. Establish a friendly, welcoming atmosphere by providing coffee, bottles of water or soda, and some bagels or cookies. A good data room will set the scene for a quick, painless diligence process and have a tremendous impact on getting you the deal you want.

WORKSHEET 8A

Sample Confidentiality Agreement (Template)

The following is an example of an NDA I often use. Have your attorney review it to make sure it's right for you.

RECIPROCAL NONDISCLOSURE AGREEMENT

THIS NONDISCLOSURE AGREEMENT is entered into as of the ______ day of ______________, __________, by and between (BUYER COMPANY NAME & ADDRESS) hereinafter referred to as ______________________________________ and (SELLER COMPANY NAME & ADDRESS) hereinafter referred to as ______________________________________.

Each party hereto (individually a "Party" and together, the "Parties") has requested and/or will learn from the other party hereto, its subsidiaries or affiliates (collectively, the "Disclosing Party"), from or through the Disclosing Party's employees, officers, directors, independent contractors, agents or representatives, information, both orally and in writing, concerning the intellectual property and/or business of the Disclosing Party and/or current or potential customers of the Disclosing Party, including, without limitation, discoveries, ideas, concepts, know-how, techniques, designs, specifications, drawings, blueprints, tracings, diagrams, models, samples, flow charts, data, computer programs, source code, software, disks, diskettes, tapes, customer lists, customer addresses, products and services provided to specific customers, sales volumes, customer pricing, equipment specifications, locations and use, network configurations, capacities and capabilities, current or prospective relationship with vendors and independent contractors (including, without limitation, information regarding the types of products and services contracted for and the cost of such products and services to the Disclosing Party), implementation of technology, data and programs, finance, sales, marketing, and development of Internet, telecommunication and related technology and services. Such information, in whole or in part, together with analyses, compilations, programs, reports, proposals, studies, or any other documentation, prepared by the Disclosing Party or the other Party (the "Receiving Party"), as the case may be, which contain or otherwise reflect or make reference to such information, whether or not specifically marked as confidential by the Disclosing Party, are hereinafter referred to as "Confidential Information."

All Confidential Information is deemed proprietary to the Disclosing Party. Accordingly, as a condition precedent to entering into discussions, and in connection with any business relationship, whether formal or informal, which is or may be established between the Parties, the Receiving Party hereby agrees, as set forth below, to hold Confidential Information of the Disclosing Party, whether furnished before, on, or after the date of this agreement, in the strictest confidence and not to disclose such information to anyone except as otherwise provided for in this agreement.

1. *Confidential Information; marking* The Disclosing Party hereby agrees that all Confidential Information will be marked as "Confidential."

2. *Use of Confidential Information* The Receiving Party agrees that the Confidential Information will be used solely for the purpose of evaluating a potential transaction between the Parties and in connection with a business relationship, whether formal or informal, which is or may be established between the Parties, and not for any other purpose, except as otherwise agreed by the Parties in writing.

3. *Ownership of Confidential Information* The Receiving Party acknowledges that the Disclosing Party claims the Confidential Information as its sole and exclusive property (or that the Disclosing Party is a valid licensee of such information) and that the Receiving Party shall not have any right, title, or interest in or to such Confidential Information except as expressly provided in this agreement.

4. *Disclosure of Confidential Information* The Receiving Party agrees to hold in the strictest confidence and not to disclose to anyone for any reason Confidential Information of the Disclosing Party; provided, however, that:

   (a) such Confidential Information may be disclosed to the officers, directors, employees, agents, or representatives (collectively, "Representatives") of the Receiving Party on a "need to know" basis for the purpose of evaluating a potential transaction between the Parties or in connection with a business relationship, whether formal or informal,

WORKSHEET 8A

Sample Confidentiality Agreement (Cont.)

which is or may be established between the Parties, on the condition that (i) each such Representative will be informed of the confidential nature of such Confidential Information and will agree to be bound by the terms of this agreement and not to disclose such Confidential Information to any other person and (ii) each Party agrees to accept full responsibility for any breach of this agreement by that Party's Representatives; and

(b) Confidential Information of the Disclosing Party may be disclosed by the Receiving Party upon the prior written consent of the Disclosing Party.

5. *Disclosure of Discussions* Each Party agrees not to disclose, and will direct its Representatives not to disclose, to any person that discussions or negotiations are taking place between the Parties unless otherwise required by law or upon the prior written consent of the other Party. This paragraph applies, without limitation, to any use, other than strictly internal use, by a Party of the other Party's name and marks.

6. *Return of Confidential Information* The Receiving Party agrees, upon the request of the Disclosing Party, to promptly deliver to the Disclosing Party (or, with the Disclosing Party's consent, destroy) the originals and all copies of the Disclosing Party's Confidential Information then in the Receiving Party's possession or control, including, without limitation, the portion of the Confidential Information that consists of analyses, compilations, programs, reports, proposals, studies, or other documentation prepared by a Receiving Party or its Representatives.

7. *Limitations on Confidential Information* The term "Confidential Information" does not include any information which:

(a) is or becomes generally available to or known by the public (other than as a result of a disclosure directly or indirectly by the Receiving Party);
(b) is independently developed by the Receiving Party without breach of this agreement;
(c) is lawfully received by the Receiving Party without restriction from a third party who obtained the Confidential Information other than as a result of a breach of any confidentiality obligation; or
(d) is disclosed by the Receiving Party pursuant to judicial action or governmental regulations, provided that the Receiving Party notifies the Disclosing Party prior to such disclosure and the Receiving Party cooperates with the Disclosing Party in the event that the Disclosing Party elects legally to contest and avoid such disclosure.

8. *Term* The terms and conditions of this agreement shall continue for a period of three years from the date hereof; provided, however, that the Parties agree that the obligations of confidentiality hereunder shall survive such term.

9. *Specific Performance* The Parties acknowledge and agree that the rights being protected by the terms of this agreement are of a special, unique, unusual, and extraordinary character, which gives them a particular value, and that the breach of any provision of this agreement may cause irreparable injury and damage to the non-breaching Party. In such event, the non-breaching Party shall be entitled to require specific performance of all of the acts and the undertakings required of the breaching Party hereunder and to obtain injunctive and other equitable relief in any court of competent jurisdiction to prevent the violation or threatened violation of any of the provisions of this agreement. Neither this paragraph 9 nor any exercise by the non-breaching Party of its right to equitable relief or specific performance herein granted shall constitute a waiver by the non-breaching Party of any other rights which it may have to damages or other relief.

10. *Enforceability* If any of the provisions contained in this agreement is held to be unenforceable, in whole or in part, by a court of competent jurisdiction, the Parties agree to be bound by all other provisions of this agreement.

WORKSHEET 8A

Sample Confidentiality Agreement (Cont.)

11. *Successors* The Parties agree that this agreement shall be binding upon the successors and assigns of such Party and shall inure to the benefit of, and be enforceable by, such successors and assigns, and any officers or directors thereof.

12. *Waiver* The Parties agree that a Party's failure at any time to require performance of any provision of this agreement shall in no way affect such Party's right at a later time to enforce the same. No waiver by a Party of a breach of a term contained in this agreement, whether by conduct or otherwise, in any one or more instances, shall be deemed to be or construed as a further or continuing waiver of such breach of any other term of this agreement.

13. *Applicable Law* This agreement shall be governed by, and construed in accordance with, the laws of the State of (YOUR STATE if acceptable), without regard to its conflicts of laws provisions. Any proceeding related to this agreement shall be brought only in a court of competent jurisdiction located in the State of (YOUR STATE).

■ ■ ■

IN WITNESS WHEREOF, the parties hereto have executed this Agreement as of the date first written above:

BUYER NAME/ENTITY NAME	SELLER NAME/ENTITY NAME
By: ______________________	By: ______________________
Print Name: ______________________	Print Name: ______________________
Title: ______________________	Title: ______________________

WORKSHEET 8B

Buyer's Due Diligence List

1. CORPORATE STRUCTURE

- ☐ Capitalization table of seller to show equity ownership
- ☐ Seller's corporate structure chart
- ☐ Management organization chart
- ☐ Board of directors information

2. CORPORATE ORGANIZATION DOCUMENTS

- ☐ Seller's certificate of incorporation with amendments and bylaws
- ☐ Minutes of board of directors meetings
- ☐ Board of directors and shareholder consents
- ☐ Stock ledger

3. ACCOUNTANTS' AND AUDITORS' REPORTS AND FINANCIAL STATEMENTS

- ☐ Audited financial statements for each of the past three years
- ☐ Consolidated income statements
- ☐ Audit response letters from counsel
- ☐ Miscellaneous financial information
- ☐ Revenue recognition policy
- ☐ Pro forma projections over the next four years
- ☐ Year-end financial statistics from current year or most recent year

4. ACQUISITION DOCUMENTS

- ☐ Asset acquisitions from past ten years
- ☐ Documents related to recapitalization of seller's companies

5. CONTRACTS

- ☐ Confidentiality agreements between seller and key clients
- ☐ Sample purchase order form
- ☐ Summaries of contracts
- ☐ Operations contracts and related information
- ☐ Consulting services agreements
- ☐ Accountant's consulting documents
- ☐ Equipment leases
- ☐ Lease agreements

WORKSHEET 8B

Buyer's Due Diligence List (Cont.)

6. DEBT ARRANGEMENTS

☐ Summary of long-term debt arrangements
☐ Credit agreements

7. EMPLOYEE INFORMATION

☐ Human resources report
☐ Chart of employees by region
☐ Employee summaries (hourly versus salaried)
☐ Management information
☐ Management salary information
☐ Management organization charts
☐ Payroll information

8. EMPLOYEE BENEFITS INFORMATION

☐ Benefit summary
☐ Benefit plans and related information
☐ Sample noncompetitive and nondisclosure agreements
☐ Severance pay agreements
☐ Stock option plans
☐ Seller's executive deferred compensation plan
☐ Employee bonus information
☐ Employee disability, leave, and vacation information
☐ Sample option grants
☐ Flexible benefits plan information (Form 5500, etc.)
☐ Employee car allowance information
☐ Schedule of stock option grants
☐ Profit-sharing retirement plan

9. INTELLECTUAL PROPERTY

☐ Patent, trademark, and copyright status reports

10. INSURANCE

☐ Insurance coverage summaries
☐ Insurance information—loss summaries, etc.

11. ENVIRONMENT AND SAFETY

☐ List of issues
☐ Environmental reports (past four years)
☐ Miscellaneous environmental information

WORKSHEET 8B

Buyer's Due Diligence List (Cont.)

12. SALES INFORMATION

- ☐ Sample sales brochures and other information
- ☐ Sales-related surveys
- ☐ Business overview presentation

13. TAX MATTERS

- ☐ Historical tax information
- ☐ Tax returns
- ☐ Tax provision information (past three years)

14. REAL PROPERTY

- ☐ Lease 1 ________________________________
- ☐ Lease 2 ________________________________
- ☐ Lease 3 ________________________________
- ☐ Lease 4 ________________________________
- ☐ Lease 5 ________________________________

15. APPRAISALS OF RELEVANT PROPERTY

- ☐ Property 1 ________________________________
- ☐ Property 2 ________________________________
- ☐ Property 3 ________________________________
- ☐ Property 4 ________________________________
- ☐ Property 5 ________________________________

16. MISCELLANEOUS

- ☐ Information on pricing analysis
- ☐ Database information
- ☐ Depreciation expense reports
- ☐ Press releases
- ☐ List of top ten clients over the past three years
- ☐ Locations of inventory
- ☐ Lease obligations
- ☐ Incremental capital requests, if any
- ☐ Competitive chart and summary

CHAPTER 9

Popping the Cork

THE VERY FIRST TIME I was set to close on the sale of my company, I walked into the conference room of the firm that was acquiring my business, with my attorney, and what did I see? Spread out along the entire perimeter of a huge conference table were what seemed like one thousand piles of documents neatly organized and ready for me to sign. I've got to admit, I was a little freaked out. There was something about signing my name to all those copies of all those documents in all those piles that made me feel like a sheep in a wolf's den. I wasn't at all prepared for that sight. I felt as if I were about to sign my life away.

Fast-forward a bunch of years and many acquisitions later. Now this process is second nature to me. I understand the need for each of the documents, that they merely codify (or make legal) all aspects of the deal, the representations made, the terms of payment, and much more.

Selling a business is like selling a home: In both cases all the negotiations culminate in a closing. This event, although seemingly a huge deal, is usually a mere formality that takes place at the offices of the buyer or the buyer's attorney. You sign the purchase agreement and other binding documents; your lawyer will have negotiated the terms of the major documents beforehand and will review each of them with you before the closing. If cash is involved, the funds are transferred with a wire transfer or a check; I prefer wire transfers so I can earn interest immediately. If stock is issued, you'll receive the necessary documentation as well.

The Closing Lineup

Take a look at the following list of closing documents below and read the brief explanation of some of the less obvious ones. I picked these documents randomly; each transaction is unique, so the package of documents you sign will probably differ in some ways—there will probably be less than what is included here. I am using these to show you what some of your documents might be and to illustrate the level of detail you will be dealing with at your closing. Familiarize yourself with these, and get your attorney's advice; this will prepare you for the closing and give you confidence in what might otherwise be a pretty scary process. (At the end of this chapter, you will find a worksheet listing of these documents that you can tear out and carry with you as needed.)

- **Asset or stock purchase agreement.** This is the biggie. It is signed by both parties and contains the details of your agreement, including the representations and warranties. Specific schedules (some examples are noted below) will also tie to this agreement.
- **Purchase agreement schedules.** The ones listed below are some examples of what you will see at an actual closing. Typically these are signed by the seller, but some are signed by the buyer as well. The seller should have discussed these items with the buyer before the closing, so there should be no surprises. The goal of the schedules is to disclose material facts about the company and its parties. Read them all; they tie to the representations and warranties, and default or incorrect statements here can cost you money and peace of mind later. Typically the schedules will call out exceptions or list the items omitted from the transaction as spelled out in the purchase agreement.

Only after all these documents are signed and the money is transferred should you consider the deal complete. But once that has happened, it's time to shake hands—and pop the cork! You did it!

WORKSHEET 9A

Closing Documents

You are not ready to seal the deal until you have addressed and signed off on all of these elements.

1. ☐ Asset or stock (if corporation)
   ☐ Purchase Agreement (Both parties)
2. Schedules:
   ☐ Employment agreement
   ☐ Equipment – tie into rep and warranty under the agreement
   ☐ Inventory
   ☐ List of receivables good valid and receivable – signed by buyer/seller or both
   ☐ Deposits
   ☐ Prepaid Assets
   ☐ Contracts
   ☐ Customer Lists
   ☐ Intellectual Property
   ☐ Transfer of Intellectual Property
   ☐ Authorizations
   ☐ Memberships
   ☐ Excluded Personal Property
   ☐ Excluded Accounts Receivable
   ☐ Trade Accounts Payable
   ☐ Vacation Accrued
   ☐ Customers Excluded from Litigation
   ☐ Title to Acquired Assets
   ☐ Oral or Written Contracts; Defaults
   ☐ Litigation
   ☐ Employees; Employee Plans
   ☐ Employee Handbooks
   ☐ Related Transactions
   ☐ Product Liability
   ☐ Allocation of Purchase Price
3. ☐ Promissory Note
4. ☐ Bill of Sale
5. Assignment and Assumption Agreement – assuming liabilities like trade payables and indemnify seller
6. ☐ Consulting Agreement – employment agreement
7. ☐ Closing Statement-RESPA
8. ☐ Lease
9. ☐ Secretary's Certificate – Buyer
   ☐ Board of Directors' Resolutions
10. ☐ Certificate of Good Standing – Buyer
11. ☐ Certificate of Good Standing – Seller
12. ☐ Secretary's Certificate – Seller
    ☐ Board of Directors' Resolutions
    ☐ Shareholders' Resolutions
    ☐ Certified Articles of Incorporation; and
    ☐ By-Laws
13. ☐ Articles of Amendment – Seller (Name Change)
14. ☐ Articles of Amendment – Buyer (Name Change)
15. ☐ Cancellation of Assumed Names
16. ☐ Assumption of Assumed Names
17. ☐ Board of Directors Resolution – Name Assumption – Buyer
18. ☐ Trademark Assignment
20. ☐ Guaranty
21. ☐ Escrow Agreement

PART THREE

Going for the Limit

■■■

CHAPTER TEN
Get the Premium Price
Page 113

CHAPTER ELEVEN
Communicate Effectively
Page 125

CHAPTER TWELVE
Protect Your Employees and Yourself
Page 137

CHAPTER THIRTEEN
Plan for Succession
Page 143

CHAPTER 10

Get the Premium Price

WE'VE BEEN CONCENTRATING ON THE BASIC THINGS you have to know and the actions you need to take to sell your company: getting it in top shape, making the buyer comfortable, putting together your team, positioning your business for the sale, negotiating effectively, and the like. Now we turn to the turbocharged version—how to get top dollar.

Second Time's the Charm

In its twelve years of operation, Vogel Personal Coaching had developed a loyal clientele. It had grown so much that founder Margheta Vogel had to hire and train four additional life coaches to help her keep up with the demand. Together they worked to enhance the happiness of their customers by helping them identify and focus on their personal priorities. Margheta loved her work, especially when she saw how it improved the lives of her clients. She used a unique, specialized coaching style, working with clients individually to develop the perfect training for their specific priorities.

At this point in her life, Margheta wanted to make a change of her own, which is why she decided to sell Vogel Personal Coaching. She wasn't sure how to go about this, but after considering the various possibilities, she contacted another personal coaching team and proposed a merger. She would move her practice into the buyer's offices and leave the business after a year. There were offers and counteroffers on sell price and terms, but she couldn't get the prospect to agree to the valuation she thought her company was worth, and negotiations ended without a deal.

This is when I was brought into the picture. I spent some time snooping around Vogel Personal Coaching and asked Margheta what she thought the company was worth. She told me that Vogel had 106 clients, annual sales of $420,000, and profits of $170,000, which she took out of the business at the end of each year. Margheta was looking for a sell price of $800,000, which came to about 4.7 times one year's profits.

Every business has untapped value that can be identified and leveraged to increase the sale price.

We then discussed her first attempt at selling the business, which had yielded a buy offer of less than $340,000 to be paid over several years—a far cry from the price she was hoping for. When I asked how she had presented her case for the $800,000 sell price (which at the time seemed to me a bit high), she told me that she was giving them her book of clients, of which she figured about half would switch to the new owners and their location. I pointed out that with an expected 50 percent drop in business, her price was actually more than nine times future earnings. She countered that the new owners would be able to sell her old clients their own line of products and services, which she didn't offer, and that reducing rent by combining offices would offset some of the lost customer revenues.

I stopped her at that point. I had heard enough to know that although she would be able to sell her business, there was no way she would get anywhere near what she was asking. To get that price, she would have to make major changes in the way she was identifying and presenting the true value that resided within her company. So here's what we did: We took inventory.

No, not that kind of inventory. What I'm talking about is an activity that identifies and builds value in your business. This activity utilizes my Value Identification Process—VIP for short. Catchy, huh? Every good business, of course, has products and services, but it also has processes and other intangibles, such as the unique way it operates, the particular processes it uses to do the things it does, and the ways it keeps its customers loyal, that yield intrinsic value. The purpose of my VIP is to identify and highlight those features so that they are recognized and valued by current and prospective customers, the employees who serve them, and—in this case—any company that is considering acquiring the business.

We wrote down all the unique processes that Margheta used to customize the experience for her clients—such things as a face-to-face meeting in which Vogel experts would walk through a twenty-point evaluation, special techniques for mental goal-setting, and a set of exercises tailored to the client's specific needs. We grouped these services into a suite, branded it with a distinctive and memorable name, then trademarked it: The Vogel Factor.

This was a major step in maximizing the value of the company. It allowed Margheta to show and sell something recognizable and valuable to the buyers, a set of features that distinguished Vogel from her competitors. We created a simple but beautiful one-page marketing piece outlining the steps and benefits of The Vogel Factor. Whoever acquired Vogel would get The Vogel Factor as well, which could then be used to attract more customers.

We used this process again and again across every aspect of Margheta's business and came up with seven additional processes that we were able to isolate, formulate into a step-by-step explanation, and brand with a distinctive name. These processes ranged from the individual exercises the clients were given to do, to the physical and mental goal-setting methods that were already highlighted under the umbrella trade name The Vogel Factor, to the methods used for getting and keeping new customers, such as Vogel's referral and frequent-user programs. We dug in and formulated, then implemented, a plan to develop a client database, complete with marketing data accumulated as the client took more and more classes. This database (also branded) was to be featured as well in the value discussion of the business. These proprietary processes are your Unique Selling Propositions (USPs).

PLANNING FOR GOLD FORMULA:

CREATIVITY IN IDENTIFYING VALUE + BRANDING =

BIGGER MONEY FOR YOU

Why did we apply the Value Identification Process to Margheta's business? Simple. In order to realize the highest possible sell price, you have to get the buyer to see all the things that it gains from the purchase of your business—in addition to the expected financial advantages and the obvious products and services. These tangible and intangible extras—your processes and USPs—are the things you draw the buyer's attention to by branding them.

Once we had done this, we moved on to the next step of our VIP—creating a vision for the company. Even though Margheta wasn't going to be part of the business after the first year, it was vital that she pass on some great ideas for the future of the business, both as the independent company it was and as part of another entity, as it would be if the deal went through.

Now, this sounds like a lot of work, doesn't it? Well, there's some work involved, but most of all, it's creative, and actually a lot of fun. The exercise helps you see your business in the most positive light; you will gain a new appreciation for the things that make your business uniquely valuable to your customers and to a potential buyer. What's more, there are few things you can do that will be more effective in bringing you a top sell price, and knowing this should make you even happier and even more creative.

If you expect a buyer to pay a premium for your business, you have to make them understand and believe they're getting something extra special.

Developing premium aspects to your business using USPs and value branding is one thing; communicating them to a potential buyer, having them acknowledged, and getting credit for them—that's the trick in getting top price. If you expect a buyer to pay a premium for your business, you have to make them understand and believe they're getting something that is really very special.

About nine months after her first attempt at selling, Margheta was ready to try again. This time, though, she felt she had a completely different business. Vogel Personal Coaching did the exact same things as before, but the time we spent identifying and branding the company's value points prepared Margheta well for the negotiations and gave her confidence. She was able to convince her next prospect of the true value of the company, and three months later she completed her sale—for $1.2 million!

Value Identification Process (VIP)

Want another example of effective USP development? Consider my Value Identification Process. I branded my proprietary method "VIP" to communicate the value it adds to the sell process and to make it memorable. It makes my services more valuable than simply my showing up and saying, "Let's try this," and "Let's try that." It shows that there's a well-thought-out system involved.

The VIP is a seven-part process that I've used countless times with great success. Follow along and implement these procedures in your business right away. You'll be amazed at how much they help not only your sell price but your entire outlook for your business as well. Below are the steps; use Worksheet 10A to record your results.

1. **Identify and develop USPs.** Unique selling propositions are the things that distinguish your company from your competition. The purpose of this step is to identify both the obvious and the hidden value areas within your company, the way we did with Margheta at Vogel Personal Coaching. List and describe every process, area of expertise, uniqueness, or method involved in running your business, from every possible angle: Operation, administration, and sales. Consider finance and human resources: Maybe you have a highly effective way of identifying and retaining valuable employees that might be useful to a buyer. (Keep these processes handy for your succession plan, which we'll cover in chapter 13.)

I like to start with sales. Do you maintain a customer database? If so, write that down. Do you use a systematic process for closing a sale? What else goes on in sales that's unique or effective? Move on to the contract stage. Anything unique here? Do you offer an incentive to get the client to countersign and return the agreement quickly? List that, too.

Next, operations. Walk through each step of your company's processes from contract through delivery; include anything possible, such as how you select your vendors, search for the most effective pricing, buy your materials, ensure quality control, guarantee shipping—any process at all that you use systematically and successfully.

Look deep into your business and search out the nuggets. Be creative. Get your people involved, the ones who are constantly applying and improving these processes. Emphasize the importance of USPs and branding for the business as a whole. This is something that every business should be doing anyway, not only for marketing to customers but for maintaining employees' focus on continual improvement and pride of ownership. Delegate responsibility for this to individuals in various departments; it will help get them more involved in their piece of the business. If you employ only a few people, get everyone involved. (For much more on how to develop your USPs, see my previous book, *Be the Elephant*.)

More than 90% of businesses do not identify and communicate all of their available value.

2. **Select your USPs.** Now that you have a list of potential USPs, the next step is to select the ones that make sense for both your business and the sale.

For the business, you'll want to include every USP that gives you a competitive advantage, addresses any shortfall in the business, or accentuates any advantage you have in the marketplace—product superiority, customer service applications, sales closing processes, database compilation, marketing processes, to mention but a few. These will, of course, be communicated to the prospect, but they are also vital to the development and growth of your business in the long run.

For the sale, you'll want to proceed with every USP that arguably gives you a competitive advantage or that focuses on efficiency: Processes that a buyer might be able to use in its current business, practices that demonstrate that you and your team are savvy and professional. These might include procedures for buying goods and services, quality control assurance measures, hiring processes, and more.

3. **Brand your USPs.** Branding a process, product, or anything else means one thing: Assigning a name to its distinct characteristics to create a clear visual understanding of what it is. Effective branding gives it life and lets others understand and visualize it quickly.

A.C.R.O.N.Y.M.S. and You

Turning your brand names into acronyms can make your USPs or other value features easier to recall and more compelling. I create and use them all the time, especially when I'm trying to highlight certain processes. It's also great within the company: It gets people using a unique internal language, which is great for continuity and helps create better team spirit. For prospects, acronyms signal the importance you place on certain functions, which encourages employees to give these areas more value.

Here are names of some of the acronyms that other people and I have created for our businesses, along with an explanation of what they represent and why we chose to use them. Most of these are simple processes or reports; the acronyms give them more credibility. I urge you to develop acronyms (with or without periods, your choice) for the important functions of your business.

ACRONYM	FULL NAME	WHY USED
CAR	Client Activity Report	Keeps clients up to speed on projects
ACE	Automated Cost Efficiency	Lets customers know how much they're saving by using automated equipment
FIT	Finite Indicator Technology	Shoe store device to determine the best brand of gym shoe for the customer
PIT	Priority Inquiry Technology	Seating technology used by ticket broker that guarantees the best seating available at over a hundred venues
VIP	Value Identification Process	Steve Kaplan's method for finding and communicating value residing within a business

For each USP that makes it past step 2, use the USP description from step 1 to name it. This is the really fun part, your chance to be creative, to play outside the fence. Think of who is going to read, see, or hear your new brand; put yourself in her place. Does the name tell her the meaning? Does it say what you're trying to say? If so, you're done. If not, keep on thinking.

Get others involved in naming your USPs. Explain what message you're trying to convey. Make it a challenge; a free lunch for whoever comes up with the winning name.

You might consider trademarking the names you particularly like, but in many cases a formal trademark application is not necessary as long as you can prove when you started using the names. Check with your attorney.

4. **Create a descriptor sheet.** Once you've identified, explained, and named your first USP, you're ready to put it together into a piece that communicates what it's all about. Depending on your promotional needs and targets, this piece can range from a simple outline to a full-color marketing or sell booklet. Take your strongest USP and turn it into an attractive marketing piece that you can print out for your prospective buyer. With the right software, you can do this inexpensively on your own color printer. For a real killer presentation, you can spend more money and turn to an ad agency.

5. **Create your vision.** Prepare two separate pieces to present your vision: One solely for your business, another for the prospect's and your businesses combined post deal.

When preparing the vision piece for your current business, consider the following questions: What will your industry look like in the future? How do you plan to leverage the coming technologies? What is your company's strategy for dominating the industry? This is where you impress the prospect with your vision. Again, think big—don't limit yourself to current fiscal or staffing constraints. This is a "What if I had the resources?" exercise.

For the combined businesses, think of as many ways as possible that your shared customers, buying power, technical expertise, marketing programs, financial resources, and other assets can be combined to explosive effect. What strategic benefits and growth opportunities will the buyer gain by acquiring you? Prepare a forward-looking brochure for the new partnership that really wows the prospect.

With this two-pronged approach, you'll show that your company has a plan to grow on its own, but that it clearly makes more sense to grow together. Drive home this idea of a collaborative effort by using dual logos on the piece. This will reinforce the buyer's decision to acquire your company, thus making your company more attractive—and worth more. Here's the interesting part: Although you obviously don't have enough insight into the prospect's company to do an accurate job of leveraging its business for growth, the fact that you've given it some thought and may well have hit on something unforeseen will intensify the company's desire to acquire you.

6. **Communicate your message.** Having these great promotional tools is one thing; communicating them effectively to your prospect to get a premium price is something else. What's the best way to get the message across that your company is one the prospect can't do without? Actually, it's another tool, one we've already discussed.

Remember the business overview from chapter 3, "Prepare Your Company"? This is an excellent place to make your case with the USP descriptor and vision materials discussed in steps 4 and 5 above. They should appear in several places: First, in any section they apply to—for example, sales USPs in the section on sales, quality control USPs in the operational flow section. (Note: This might be a good time to review the sample business overview available on my website, *www.differencemaker.com*.)

Focus on the aspects of your business that will be of the most interest to the buyer and most likely to enhance the value of your company. The USPs should be discussed under a separate heading, such as "Intellectual Property" or "Proprietary Processes." Present them as a series of slides, or create a one-page chart listing USPs and describing them briefly. When I presented my USPs in PowerPoint, I usually showed the chart, then included the individual USP sheets in the hard copy. I also referred often to USPs by name throughout the sale process to drive the point home.

Prepare your company well in advance by creating USPs early, using the brand names in everyday business, and making sure all your people are familiar with them. Then, when your prospective buyer hears other team members referring routinely to your company's USPs, it makes a better impression of your company as a well-planned, well-organized, well-run enterprise.

7. Present the *organization*. Always talk about your company as an organization, not a small company (especially not a business run from your home); a buyer will pay more for an "organization" than for a "business." A good way to do this is to talk up your management. Use words like team and we, not I or me. Your work in steps 1–3 will also help promote the organization and team concept you're fostering.

In the next chapter, I'll discuss the importance of getting your management in front of the buyers, ideally toward the end of the diligence process when you are feeling good about the deal going through. Before that meeting, make sure that all the players in your organization are on the same page regarding the direction of the company, its strategy, their role in the organization, and anything else you think the buyer might want to discuss with them. Remember that this must align with what you've told the prospect. It should be easy; your team should know the strategy and their role in it, so all that's needed should be a recap. For business reasons alone, you should make sure to get your team aligned toward achieving your collective company goals.

WORKSHEET 10A

VIP Worksheet for USP Development

Working your way through the contract execution chain, create USPs by department. Be thorough and comprehensive. Use a new sheet for each department or function.

DEPARTMENT ______________________

Details: What is it? What does it do? Use a separate sheet if necessary.

1. ______________________
2. ______________________
3. ______________________
4. ______________________
5. ______________________
6. ______________________
7. ______________________
8. ______________________
9. ______________________
10. ______________________

SELECT YOUR USPs

1. ______________________
2. ______________________
3. ______________________
4. ______________________
5. ______________________
6. ______________________
7. ______________________
8. ______________________
9. ______________________
10. ______________________

CREATE A BRAND NAME FOR EACH USP

1. ______________________
2. ______________________
3. ______________________
4. ______________________
5. ______________________
6. ______________________
7. ______________________
8. ______________________
9. ______________________
10. ______________________

WORKSHEET 10A

VIP Worksheet for USP Development (Cont.)

Working your way through the contract execution chain, create USPs by department. Be thorough and comprehensive. Use a new sheet for each department or function.

DEPARTMENT ____________________

Details: What is it? What does it do? Use a separate sheet if necessary.

1. ____________________
2. ____________________
3. ____________________
4. ____________________
5. ____________________
6. ____________________
7. ____________________
8. ____________________
9. ____________________
10. ____________________

SELECT YOUR USPs

1. ____________________
2. ____________________
3. ____________________
4. ____________________
5. ____________________
6. ____________________
7. ____________________
8. ____________________
9. ____________________
10. ____________________

CREATE A BRAND NAME FOR EACH USP

1. ____________________
2. ____________________
3. ____________________
4. ____________________
5. ____________________
6. ____________________
7. ____________________
8. ____________________
9. ____________________
10. ____________________

CHAPTER 11

Communicate Effectively

COMMUNICATION IS, OF COURSE, the basic tool behind everything we've discussed in the book so far. Selling your company requires communication in its many forms—conversations, e-mails, telephone calls, legal documents—because that's the way ideas are exchanged. Assembling your team, negotiating, and due diligence all rest on a foundation of communication, the most powerful tool available to humans, the one that makes civilization possible. Communication is like fire: Used skillfully and purposefully, it can work wonders; out of control, it can cause grievous damage.

In this chapter we'll look into communication itself as a tool whose power must be controlled. Our focus will be on when and how to communicate the news to your employees and your customers.

As you negotiate the intricacies of the transaction, don't forget the all-important human side of the deal. What, when, and how should you tell your employees about the potential sale? On one hand, you'll want to keep quiet about the negotiations until it's time to let everyone in on the plan—but even though you've done your best to keep the news locked up, it may already have slipped out. If the cat's out of the bag, how do you control the damage? (Read chapter 14, "The 'Yak Yak' Factor," to see what can happen when you communicate or share with your team too early.)

The Company Rumor Mill

I subscribe to a need-to-know policy when selling a company: Early in the process, the only people who should hear anything at all are those who absolutely must—your attorneys, outside accountants, investment advisers and the like, who are not in your company and who are professionally obliged to maintain confidentiality.

There are two big reasons why I am so adamant about not sharing my plans to sell:

- Most deals fall through. If I tell my people I'm exploring a sale, all I do is create anxiety and make workers unhappy and unproductive for no reason.
- Unless I know exactly what the plans are for the business and its employees, discussing even the potential for a sale creates concern, which can lead to panic—the very thing that, as a leader, I need to protect them from.

Remember, there will be plenty of time to fill everyone in on your plans later. By keeping mum until the time comes to talk, you should be able to communicate under ideal conditions, when the situation best suits you and you have answers to the questions your employees are sure to ask. Typically, this time is immediately before diligence starts and after the following have occurred:

- You've had several discussions with the potential buyer.
- You've received a signed formal offer or term sheet for the business.
- You've had at least one personal meeting with the buyer at the decision-maker level (otherwise, how serious could the offer really be?).
- You've agreed on how much the business is worth.
- You've agreed on terms—cash, stock, earn-out, lump payment, and so on.
- You've determined, to the best of your ability, what effect the buyer's plans will have on your employees (which people or positions will be terminated, moved, demoted, or promoted; which offices will be closed, moved, consolidated, or expanded; or whether your operation will be left basically unchanged).
- You've agreed on a proposed closing date.

The Big Reveal

Once the deal is well under way—or once your employees have started to gossip about your plans—it's time to break the news officially. This is a "one-and-done" situation: You have only one chance to do it right, and if you screw it up, it can turn into a disaster.

At the first meeting with your staff, you should cover, at the very least, the following topics:

- **Why this acquisition makes sense for the company**
- **What effect the acquisition will have on them (based on your talks with the buyer)**
- **What your intentions are after the sale**
- **How you will work to keep distractions to a minimum**
- **Details about the rest of the process and what sort of time line they might expect**

This briefing should cover most of the concerns your people will have. Be ready to answer any other questions that come up; there will probably be some you can't answer, and you should tell your employees so. Reassure them that you'll do everything in your power to make the transition as easy and as painless as possible. Your objective is to get your crew to return to work with renewed vigor rather than contemplate abandoning what they see as a sinking ship. (Use Worksheet 11A at the end of this chapter as a general guide to what needs to be discussed.)

The following steps will help you lead your troops smoothly through the thickets of the sell process.

1. **Prepare.** Work out what you will say ahead of time; anticipate the questions that will be thrown at you and have answers for them; try to use positive answers and emphasize the upside to allay your employees' fears. Start with the list above and add as many areas as you feel necessary. Practice your speech with a spouse or trusted (non-employee) friend acting the part of a distraught employee.

2. **Be empathetic.** Ask yourself who is on the receiving end of what you're saying, and what does that person think about it. For some leaders this comes naturally, but for many it's something that requires focus and effort. Think about each comment you're going to make, every area you're going to discuss. Put yourself

in the shoes of your audience. How will they react? What will be their biggest concerns? Who will be affected secondhand? Anticipating their emotional reaction can make the difference between effective communication and a perfunctory exchange of words. Yes, you're busy and it takes time, but your ability to empathize with the audience will serve you well in both your business and your personal life. This step should transcend the initial meeting and become part of your everyday communication skills.

3. **Be visual.** Consider putting together a short (15- to 30-minute) group presentation with slides covering the various issues to be discussed. Making the presentation formal will demonstrate your genuine concern for your employees' needs. Slides are better than handouts because you won't leave anything in writing.

4. **Understand employee personalities.** As I know you're aware, you have different personality types within your company that have nothing to do with title or salary. Here's a quick guide to three that you particularly need to deal with:

Inquisitors. You'll find inquisitors in many departments but usually not in one place. Inquisitors run the grapevine and deal in gossip. They always know who's dating whom, where the holiday party is, who's having trouble at home. When you get wind of false rumors going around, but you're not ready to make a formal announcement, you can use inquisitors to disseminate the correct information to your employees. A few words dropped judiciously to a few well-chosen ears can replace bad information with good.

Influencers. Which people in your organization are the most respected, the ones other employees turn to for advice, guidance, and leadership? These people are your influencers. They are usually, but not always, your top performers in sales or operations. They may be your senior employees, key people in middle management, or even some rank-and-file people who others turn to for answers and follow in responding to anything that affects them and their career. It's vital to get them up to speed. When it's time to talk or when you've made a major decision affecting the organization, having influencers supporting you will carry the day, because others will conform to the timing of the influencers. Consider meeting with them just minutes before the company meeting.

Manage your Inquisitors, Influencers, and Rogues to maximize your employee support.

Rogues. Some employees are relatively indifferent to your company's goings-on. To them, their job is not a career but just a way to earn money. When drama and uncertainty loom on the horizon, they usually don't ask a lot of questions—but if they do, and get a lot of double-talk or B.S., they start looking for another job. These are the rogues, the ones you definitely need to keep an eye on. Many salespeople, but certainly not all, fit this profile. You can manage them if you keep your act together and always communicate honestly and straightforwardly with them.

5. **Give them the facts.** Explain to your employees why you're selling the company, what it means to them, who the buyers are, and where your company fits in.

6. **Start with a bang.** Lead off with any bombshells such as organizational changes, then alleviate stress by emphasizing why selling the company is a wise move that will benefit everyone.

7. **Give them the bad news.** If you need to make organizational changes such as layoffs, changes in sales territories, changes in compensation or bonus structures, or changes in insurance or other important employee benefits, get your facts in order as soon as possible so you can share them with your troops, first to those affected and then to the company as a whole. When all the major changes have been announced, say so, for until employees know the carnage has ended, they will feel as if targets are painted on their backs—something that can kill the business just when you need it to thrive.

8. **Explain employee positives.** The first thing you should find out and let your employees know is how the sale will benefit them. You should be able to communicate this at the drop of a hat. Any good deal will help the business grow, develop, and prosper, and this means new jobs, more money, and greater opportunity for promotion and career advancement. Why else would anyone be interested in buying your company? This should be one of the main reasons you're doing the deal. When you meet with your prospective buyers, ask them how they see the business growing and, in practical terms, what they specifically plan to do to facilitate growth. Will there be bigger, more important roles for any of your employees? An acquisition often means your departments will grow in personnel and responsibility, which means higher salaries. Will there be stock options, profit sharing, or other incentives? All of these will help smooth the transition.

After the First Meeting

Of course, things don't always work out according to plan, so you should be ready to give updates as the situation changes. As the owner, you're the person closest to the facts, so it's up to you to control the way everyone else hears about them. Here are my seven communicating "musts" that will pay off for you.

1. **Set the tone.** Deal only in facts. Don't speculate—it will just come back to bite you. When you tell your employees something, make sure you give the complete picture. If you don't yet know the key facts, you should wait to speak. If someone asks you a question and you feel you must answer, simply let him know you don't have all the details, but you'll find out and get back to him with an answer. Then do so. Quickly.

2. **Downplay your personal upside.** You're about to get wealthy (or wealthier). Although many of your employees will be happy for your fortune, it's human nature to feel a bit of envy. So don't talk about that yacht you're going to buy. Focus on the benefits for employees: A faster-growing business, more opportunities for promotion, a better retirement plan. It makes you look a lot better in their eyes, and it helps keep the business healthy.

3. **Remember the little guy.** Spend time with the rank and file. This is something you should be doing anyway, but it's even more important during the sell process. I used to learn more from a ten-minute bull session with the guys on my loading dock than I ever did from my managers. Down in the trenches is a good place to take your company's pulse. It helps you gauge morale.

4. **Mother Hen.** This is an easy one: No one talks to your employees or customers but you. The prospective buyers will have an opportunity to speak with your management team during the diligence process. Conversations with your customers come as the final step before closing and are controlled.

5. **Be solid.** Employees need stability. They will look to you for reassurance during this time of uncertainty, and if they see anxiety or concern, they will respond accordingly. Don't let emotion drive you to snap at employees or make them feel you're not in control. As with every other facet of the business, you must be solid and focused on the tasks at hand.

6. **Manage quantity of sale discussion.** Don't let talk of the sale dominate the business day. Answer questions as they come up so that employees don't waste time speculating about what's going to happen; then bring the topic back to the business at hand. Get them to focus on the business by holding regular status meetings in which employees are required to present reports and lead discussions.

7. **Remain approachable.** Stay visible and ready to talk with your employees at any time. Though not all business owners are comfortable with this, being readily available enables you to quickly defuse many potentially damaging issues and correct miscommunications. Seeing you there will cause employees to focus more on their responsibilities. If you're gone for hours at a time or habitually leave early, they will feel that you're not looking out for them, that you're mentally disengaged from the business, that you're already sailing your 100-foot yacht to your tropical island.

Breaking the News to Your Customers

Letting your clients in on the news can be nerve-wracking, mostly because you don't know how they'll take it. They might be worried that the new owners won't put their needs first and foremost. Because they're accustomed to dealing directly with you or a specific representative at your company, they may fear that the dynamics of the relationship will change, and with them the quality of service or even pricing. Or, maybe they'll be happy for you.

Whatever the issues, one thing is certain: You'll need your clients on your side. The new owner will probably expect to keep your customers coming back for your services and perhaps sell them some of its own services as well. Furthermore, most potential buyers will want to meet some of your clients as part of the due-diligence process before they finalize the terms of the purchase; I always did. This is especially true when the seller company depends on a few clients for the majority of its billings.

Whenever a prospect asks to meet with you and a client, defer it until the very end of the process—after the purchase price and terms have been settled, due diligence is otherwise complete, and you've prepped your client for the meeting. To protect yourself,

Mind the minefield. Keep your customers and your buyer apart until the very end.

limit such meetings to just a couple of clients; it's not a done deal until the purchase contract is signed. And just like your employees, you don't want to alarm your clients unnecessarily or make them think twice about continuing to give you business. (For a useful guide to this topic, see Worksheet 11B at the end of this chapter.)

Here are some things you can do to break the news as gently as possible:

- If possible, tell clients in person rather than over the phone, and certainly not via e-mail. The personal approach says you value them, and if they have objections to the sale, you'll find it easier to change their minds face-to-face.
- Develop a list of benefits clients will gain from the sale: better customer service, new services, lower prices, discounts or packages with the buyer's other products, and anything else that fits the bill. Keep this list handy to give to any interested party. For a retail business, consider posting these benefits in your store.
- If you or the person who handles their accounts plans to remain with the company, be sure to let clients know.
- If your client is a business, confide in a trusted contact and champion at the client company, tell her your plans, and ask her advice on how best to spread the word.
- If your company has achieved a preferred-supplier rating with any client, make sure that status won't lapse with a change in ownership. This will be easier if you've done your homework and cultivated a relationship with purchasing, procurement, or whoever is running the approved supplier program.
- If you and the buyer share a client, ask them for a reference. This will give you more information for positioning the news later on. If they love your buyer, things should run smoothly, but if the buyer burned them in the past, you may need to do some damage control. If possible, reassure the client that your personal relationship will remain intact; if necessary, offer to get assurances from the buyer. And have that benefits list handy. Above all, be subtle.

Don't worry. If you've done your job managing the good client relationships and handle the transition smoothly without affecting their business, your customers will be very happy for you.

Rule of Overnight

Selling your business will take you through many ups and downs, some of them intense. You'll need to avoid overreacting to these or passing them along unfiltered to your employees; keeping an even keel is more important to your company than to you personally. To damp out the drama, follow my Rule of Overnight:

Wait until the next day before reacting to any major issue pertaining to the sale.

You'll be amazed at how sleeping on it changes your perspective. And because it involves selling your business, a fresh view of the situation can make a huge difference in the bottom line.

WORKSHEET 11A

Discussion Topics for Your First Meeting

Below is a checklist to use when preparing to address the troops and to develop your company presentation on the sale. Seek to include each element from the checklist and remember to put yourself in the shoes of each employee listening to you.

THE BUYER

☐ Product and services
☐ Their background
☐ Management team
☐ Growth strategy
☐ Where does your company fit in the buyer's growth strategy?

EMPLOYEE IMPACT

☐ Overall effect on your employees
☐ Specific impact department by department
☐ Sales department impact—territories, commissions, etc.
☐ Will there be layoffs?
☐ Will departments be merging? If so, which ones and when?

WHY SELL?

☐ What is the strategic fit?
☐ Why does the deal make sense for everyone?
☐ Will there be more potential for employee growth and career expansion?
☐ Will there be more financial gain such as profit sharing, insurance, or other benefits?
☐ Why is this the "right" time to sell?

YOUR INTENTIONS

☐ What are your plans post-sale?
☐ How will you deal with transition and when will it occur?
☐ Who will lead the business if you are leaving?

THE SALE PROCESS

☐ What is the process remaining?
☐ How will you keep distractions to a minimum?
☐ Who will be involved in the sale process?

WORKSHEET 11B

Customer Communication Worksheet

Using a separate sheet for each key customer, complete the customer communication sheet and keep it with you for reference. Make and distribute copies to other employees who interact with customers so that they are better able to assist in the cohesive communication plan.

1. For each business customer, name the contact(s) and the departments they work in that will help you push the transition through its company.

Company and Department	**Communication Contacts**
____________________	____
____________________	____
____________________	____
____________________	____

2. What are the benefits of the sale to your customers?
(Better selection, pricing, customer service, money to grow with your customer, etc.)

____

____

____

____

(For individual customers, create in-store communication such as handouts or pamphlets lauding the benefits of the change in ownership.)

3. What are your plans for making the transition smooth? How will continuity be maintained in the following areas?

Customer service ____

____

____

Sales ____

____

____

Other departments or people currently interacting with customers ______________

____

____

4. What about you, the owner? Are you staying or leaving? If leaving, will employees have as much access to the new owner as they did with you? ________________________________

____

CHAPTER 12

Protect Your Employees and Yourself

I'M OFTEN ASKED, "In all the companies you've built and run, what are you most proud of?" That's an easy one. It's not the money, or the prestige, or getting to monkey around in the world's great engine of commerce. No; it's the people. What gives me the most pride and satisfaction is the two thousand-plus employees I have gotten to know, the skilled, dedicated people who made my companies run, who in fact *were* the companies. And I can honestly say that I never felt anyone quit working for me because he was unhappy or because she felt she was being treated unfairly.

So when I say that protecting your employees, and yourself in turn, is an overriding concern in a good business, I can claim credentials.

If you're like most business owners, I know that your employees occupy a special place in your heart, too, very much like a second family—in some cases, the only family. They are people we've known for a long time, people who have worked with us and shared our defeats and our triumphs, people we've watched grow up and start families of their own. As the head of this family, you don't want to see hard times come to any of them.

And now that you're selling the business, it's a bit like letting the family home be run by a stranger—one who will let some members stay on but send others out to fend for themselves. It can be a tough transition.

Giving your employees equity in their new company is a great way to boost morale and give them a financial stake in the future success of the business.

The time to consider this and act to protect your employees is not after you've signed the purchase agreement or completed your negotiations but while you're still negotiating—that's when you have the most leverage. Actions you take to protect your employees are easy gives for your buyer, because typically they aren't that expensive. In addition, the new owner will probably be looking for ways to keep the most vital and effective workers, including key management. Think about it: The last thing the new owner wants to buy is a business whose key people are bailing out. The buyer will also appreciate the fact that you're looking out for your people; that's a sign of solid leadership.

Your situation post sale will make a difference, but whether you're staying, leaving, getting paid up front, or taking an earn-out, here are factors every business owner should consider to protect and motivate employees:

Stock options. Giving your employees equity in their new company is a great way to boost morale and give them a financial stake in the future success of the business. If you have a stock option plan in place, check to see if the options automatically vest (allowing the employee to cash them in) upon a change of ownership. Either way is okay, because your goal will be to get more options for your employees. Whenever I was selling a business to a publicly traded company that had employee stock options, typically I'd ask for a pool of options that I could distribute to my employees according to their contributions, both past and future.

A little heads up here: Once your employees get their stock options, they will line up outside your office every vesting period (the time when certain percentages of the options can be sold) asking for your advice on when or whether they should sell. My advice to you is, don't go there. No one knows what's going to happen in the markets, and anything you tell an employee could prove disastrous for him, or get you in trouble for divulging non-public material information, or both. Tell him you have no more idea than he does, which when it comes to public markets, isn't too far from the truth; advise him to talk with a financial expert who can provide unbiased insight into what's happening with the company.

Profit sharing. If your company is doing well, and regardless of whether you're thinking about selling, consider starting a profit-sharing program now. If you're far along in the process, however, your prospective buyer may have a problem with it because it's an additional expense that will come out of profits, and it may interfere with the buyer's employee compensation model.

Start your profit-sharing program as early as possible, preferably long before contemplating the sale of your business. If your company is small, you might be surprised to see the economic and motivational value this has to your employees. Many financial advisers and financial institutions manage profit-sharing plans; ask for referrals from friends and associates who have experience with profit sharing, or talk with the person who does your monthly financial statements.

Exposure. Job security is high on your employees' list of concerns. Giving them a chance to show and tell the buyer what they can do will go a long way toward alleviating their anxiety. If the buyer hasn't asked for it by the time the deal is mostly done, schedule a strategy meeting; have your key management and other valuable employees there for the buyer to meet, and let them describe their jobs and responsibilities. Talk them up a bit during the meeting, giving support to their expertise.

Some buyers ask for this interaction early in the process. As a seller, I try to put it off so employees don't get false expectations and quit focusing on their work. Nor do I want my people interacting with a buyer until they've been fully briefed and all in sync with the rest of the selling team; there usually isn't time for this until the end. I tell the buyer I want my management to stay focused on business. The buyer must, and usually does, respect that position.

Credit. When you're telling the buyer about the successes of your organization, your management team, your department heads, your growth strategy, or any other company initiatives, give the people responsible for those achievements more than their share of credit for being smart, hard-working, and resourceful. Your sales manager "has a deep understanding of the marketplace"; your IT guy "knows database architecture inside out." This will promote retention, raise morale, and help communicate the "organization" feel you're trying to convey.

Share the wealth. You're going to make a bundle from the sale; there are people who have worked for you for years, who have done more to make your company a success than you could ever have expected. Now is the time to reward them by sharing some of your windfall.

That's right, I'm suggesting that you give away money when you don't have to. Money can't buy everything, but it sure goes a long way toward reaffirming your loyalty to your employees—and gaining theirs in return. There's no need to go overboard, but someone who has been with you through thick and thin for ten years and hasn't been given a piece of the company should, in my opinion, receive something from the sale. It's the right thing to do, it's good karma, and you'll be amazed at how much it will bring you in return. Word gets around, and you'll have hordes of great people signing up for your next bold venture. These will be happy, capable people who would rather work for you than compete with you.

An organization in which everyone is loyal and driven benefits everybody.

Fight for them. When companies merge, positions are often cut for efficiency. Your buyer may have a history of downsizing acquisitions or may have explicitly told you it was planning to cut jobs in your company. This is the time to go to the mattresses for your people. Point out that your best managers and workers are essential to your operations; suggest that they might profitably replace underperforming employees in the buyer's company. Try to negotiate a "hands off" policy that would protect them from layoffs for, say, one year; that would give your people enough time to show what they've got and dazzle the buyer.

A Bit for Everyone

DataBit was a database software company with annual sales topping $6 million, of which $4 million was profit. How's that for margin? I sold it to a pretty big player as an earn-out based on nine times average earnings for the previous year, the current year, and next three years. There would be a $5 million payment up front; more substantial amounts would arrive in installments based on earnings at specific times, with the final, true-up payment due in three years. The final price figured to be somewhere between $25 million and $40 million—and if the next two years were blockbusters, the sky was the limit.

The company had only seventeen employees in its four departments, and each department head had been crucial to DataBit's success. If the sellers expected to clean up in the earn-out, it could not afford to lose any of the leadership, nor the rainmakers in sales.

The challenge would be to keep them engaged and motivated after the sale and at least through the three-year earn-out period, especially since none of them shared in the ownership. Here's how we proceeded to meet that challenge:

- **Employment agreements.** Before the sale I rewrote the employment agreements for a four-year period—one year beyond the earn-out. These were "at will" agreements—they could be terminated for any reason by either side—but I included a severance package in the event that the new buyer wanted to get rid of them for no reason. This gave the key personnel some security, which they were thankful for.
- **Control.** I negotiated hard to retain control during the earn-out period. With our compensation based on future profits, we could hardly turn decision making over to those who would be paying us, could we? This let us do what we had to do to keep our employees happy and maximize profits. It's an important point: Never hand the buyer the rope to hang you with.
- **Performance bonuses.** Since DataBit's owners valued the contributions of key employees highly, it was easy for me to persuade them to set up a bonus structure that would reward employees for even higher performance during the three years of the earn-out. Bonuses would be paid by the sellers from their up-front $5 million, based on achievement of specific profit levels. Thus, every dollar the previous owners expected to pay in bonuses—as much as $1 million—would come back nine times in the final payout (earn-out multiple). The old owners would potentially benefit big-time, and since the bonus money was put up by the old owners, the new owners would not be penalized.
- **Retention bonuses.** In addition to the performance bonuses, we established a retention bonus pool—$1 million placed in escrow by the old owners—from which employees would be rewarded with predetermined bonuses for staying with the company the full four years (one year longer than the earn-out period).

After the three-year earn-out period, the owners were paid the balance of their monies from the sale. The final price turned out to be—hold on to your hat—$49 million! So after giving $2 million to the key managers, the owners divvied up $47 million. I'd say that $2 million spent on keeping the employees protected, motivated, and happy more than paid off, wouldn't you?

INVEST IN SUCCESS:

EMPLOYEE COMPENSATION
+
EMPLOYEE EFFORT =

BIGGER MONEY FOR YOU

CHAPTER 13

Plan for Succession

A SUCCESSION PLAN IS AN OUTLINE of actions to be taken in the event that your company is unexpectedly deprived of its leadership. It details how your business would be run, and potentially who would be in charge, in the event that you or other key people (employees, suppliers, or anyone else) suddenly became ill, incapacitated, or worse. It's an operational insurance policy of sorts that you hope you never need.

Here's a way to picture it: Think of yourself as an airline pilot, and your succession plan as an emergency operations plan for the airliner you're flying. If for some reason you collapse at the controls, first you want the autopilot to keep the plane flying on a safe and steady course for the time being; then you want your copilot to take control as soon as possible to make the human decisions that will bring your plane and its passengers to a safe landing.

In terms of your company, the autopilot is the combination of personnel and processes you've set up that will keep the company operating normally from day to day as long as conditions don't change. The copilot is your second in command, or perhaps several top managers, who are empowered to make decisions when they are needed to handle emergencies or adapt to changing circumstances. If you're going to be permanently out of the picture, you need to make sure the people who replace you are people who you know can keep the company healthy and growing.

Now let's look at it from the buyer's side. Suppose you're the president of a large company who's thinking of buying the plane and the services of its crack pilot, Smilin' Jack, and you're taking a demonstration flight. You know Smilin' Jack to be a righteous airplane jockey, with a reputation as someone who can fly through the nastiest weather with the most valuable cargo (humans) and get there on time. But now that you've climbed aboard and strapped yourself in the third seat, you notice that ol' Smilin' is firing up the engines without using a preflight safety checklist.

This worries you; one thing you know is that a good pilot doesn't trust his memory or other people, such as mechanics, in determining whether the plane is ready for flight, because it's a very complicated machine and a single defect overlooked could spell disaster. You ask him, nervously, "Don't you have a preflight checklist?"

More than 90% of businesses do not have a succession plan in place. That's crazy.

"Nah. Plane's in great shape. Greasy Joe looked it over yesterday."

"But what if something's not working properly, and you don't find out until it's too late?" you say.

"Hey, no sweat. Never had a problem I couldn't handle."

"Well, what if you get to cruise altitude and discover the autopilot isn't working?"

"Never use an autopilot," he says. "I like to stay in control at all times."

Then you notice something else: "Hey, where's our copilot?"

Smilin' Jack looks at you over his shoulder and grins. "We don' need no stinkin' copilot," he says, flipping switches as he taxis merrily away from the hangar.

Now, ask yourself: Would you hire Smilin' Jack? Not if you like your top executives and their families. He may be the greatest jet jockey to walk across the tarmac, but the moment you see how he runs his business with no thought to what would happen if he dropped dead at the throttle, you lose respect for his organization. If you're smart, you'll go looking for an air charter service with a pilot whose plane and passengers will end up safely on the ground if he has bad clams for lunch. And if you're *really* smart, you'll go looking right now, before this guy takes off.

Two Insurance Policies in One

As you can readily see, there's an operational reason for having a succession plan, and there's a selling-your-business reason. The operational reason is simply to create an "insurance" policy for your company in the event that circumstances keep you from being at the controls. Knowing that your company will keep functioning in any event will give you, your employees, your charities, your family, and everyone else involved enormous peace of mind. It's also reassuring to your financial backers, suppliers, vendors, and customers if you're out of the picture temporarily. Some company heads might want to be thought indispensable, but the wise leader prefers to take pride in crafting an organization that will operate in his absence; in doing so, it serves as a living tribute to his genius.

Sometimes if you take the right step back, your business can move forward.

The other reason to have a succession plan is to reassure your buyer. If you want to get the top price for your business, you need to show that the business can thrive without you. One of the best ways to get that point across is to share your succession plan with your prospect—at the right time, of course. The mere fact that you have a succession plan speaks volumes to a buyer. It says that you are the kind of business owner who actually spends time thinking about the future of your business. If you were a buyer, wouldn't you prefer this kind of owner over one who stays at the controls every single minute, hurtling through the sky day after day without regard for tomorrow or the big "What if"?

Creating Your Succession Plan

One of the great things about creating a succession plan for your business is that the very act of doing it—walking through, thinking about, processing, and streamlining important aspects of your business—will actually enhance the effectiveness, and thus the value, of your business. In the pages that follow, I'll lead you through the process of asking questions about your business, then through the creation of formal processes that crystallize the way you do things. Use Worksheet 13A as a guide and a record for creating a succession plan. Remember to brand the processes you identify (as we discussed in chapter 10, "Get the Premium Price"). Every aspect of the succession plan should be formalized, regardless of the size of your business.

THE SECRET OF YOUR SUCCESSION

The Business Hierarchy with You

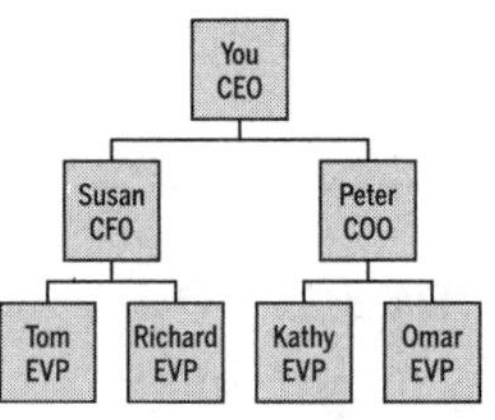

The Business Hierarchy without You

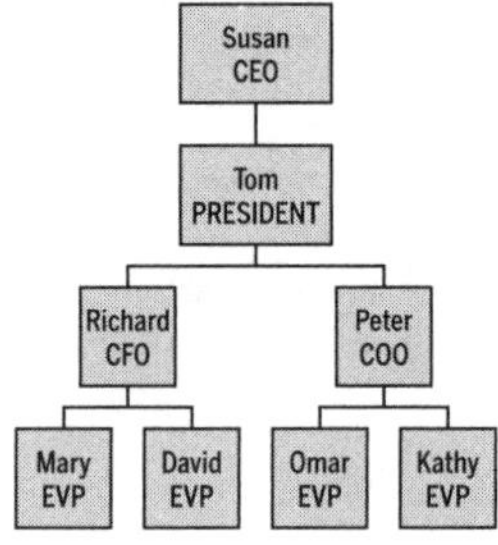

Below are eight key actions you should take in creating your succession plan. Read through them first, then use the worksheet at the end of the chapter to develop your own plan.

1. **Involve managers or other key employees.** No one says you have to create the succession plan all by yourself. You've got a company full of people who know how it works and what goes where. In fact, it will actually help your department heads if you ask them to think about and write down how they do the things they do in running their departments. Ask them to list the processes they manage and how they manage each one—employees, suppliers, technologies, etc. Once they've described these tasks, ask them to think of ways to streamline the processes to make them more efficient and thus more profitable for the business. To make things easier and more consistent, I've provided Worksheet 13B for you to use as a template.

This procedure is similar to what the leading efficiency consultants do for a company, but in this case you're asking your own leadership to identify and streamline their departments' processes. Even a small business has many processes—just fewer people performing them, which makes the processes even more important for your business to identify, describe, and streamline. You should start with the processes you've developed in chapter 10, then expand to include key inner workings of the various departments. Ask them to utilize a process chain or diagrams to make the process easier to visualize. Once you know what the processes are and who's doing what, you'll be equipped to deal with any personnel misfortunes.

2. **Create a user's guide.** Once you've identified and described your work processes, the next step is to aggregate the various process plans from your department leaders and key employees to create an operating manual for your business. Parts of this manual can be used to train new hires; even if it's not used for that purpose, it's useful to review it at intervals to see if new technologies or other developments suggest ways to simplify and streamline.

3. **Create an organization chart.** Chances are only fifty-fifty that your company has an organization chart. If you don't have one, you need to make one; it's one of those elementary things that a potential buyer will assume you have, if you're a company that has got its act together. A good organization chart is a visual map of your company's management structure; it includes all departments, names, titles, and reporting structures. Create one chart for the

current business (after streamlining), and another showing how you would wish the company to be run in your absence.

4. **Review operating agreements.** If you have a partner or partners, make sure the language of the sale agreement reflects your succession wishes. If it doesn't, sit down with your partners and create or amend the agreement.

5. **Review customer lists and contacts.** Who are your biggest customers? Who takes care of them in sales? In customer service? If you haven't done so already, create a customer database, complete with contact information. This is valuable not only for direct marketing, but for your successor as well. It will also help you get a better price when you sell the company.

6. **Include replacing key management.** What would you do if your top sales rep, office manager, vice president of operations, or other key employee became seriously ill or was otherwise lost to the business? This is what you must plan for. Take some time and write down critical personnel losses that might happen, then develop a plan to handle each contingency.

7. **Divest yourself of the business.** Now we get to the hard part. It's tough to pull yourself out of the business, but it's the most important part of the succession plan, because providing for that possibility has the most impact on both the operation of your current business and its sale to a new owner.

In many companies, including many of mine in the past, the business owner is deeply involved in many aspects of the business. For example, it's not unusual for a business owner to bring in the bulk of the sales during the day, then make the operating decisions at night; I did this for many years. Your business might be growing and operating well now, but trouble could be lurking down the road. Why?

- Your company's potential is limited; there are only so many hours in the day, and you can do only so much.
- By tying yourself so tightly to your business, you're making it almost impossible for a buyer to let you step away post purchase.
- Buyers will try to undervalue your business. If they buy you, they will have to give you a ton of money to stay on because you're essential, but they will end up with little flexibility or leverage for carrying out their own plans. If you get cranky and decide to do things your way, there won't be much they can do to get you to comply.

- You're taking a huge risk; if you get sick or incapacitated, poof! It could all vanish overnight.
- You're limiting your own potential. You can't pause and take a breath; you can't step back and evaluate your business; you've got no time to think about larger, strategic roles, new ventures, or even personal adventure and growth, for that matter. That was where I was—until I decided to remove myself from the business. When I finally did, that was when I started to thrive personally.

8. **Seek outside counsel.** Ask your attorney about estate laws in your part of the world and how they relate to succession. For example: What would happen to your shares on your demise? Would they go to your significant other, your kids, or a designated hitter to be named later? What would be the tax impact? Remember, plan before the problem.

Revisit your succession plan regularly and make sure it's kept up to date; re-evaluate and adjust as necessary every six to twelve months. The good news is that once you've done the work of creating a plan, updating it is a snap. An hour's work will give you peace of mind for the whole year.

One-Man Show

Business was great. Our annual sales had boomed to $10 million, with profits of $3 million and plenty more business ripe for the picking. Not bad for a company that I had started only three years earlier.

But I was ready to bail. After thirty-six-odd months of seven-day, hundred-hour weeks, I knew the time had come to let go. I had other things I wanted to do, and one of those things was to go global by selling the business to a giant multinational.

The problem was that I was bringing in 90 percent of the sales myself, so I was hostage to the business. I didn't even have time to look around for a buyer, much less get things tidied up and put away for a sale.

So here's what I did.

I hired four ace sales reps and trained them to sell to the four divisions of the giant packaged goods company that accounted for 70 percent of my company's sales. Every week I would trek to this company, bringing along my four new hires. I would take one to meet with the food division, another to household, the third rep to personal care, and the fourth to over-the-counter medicines. I handled most of the selling at first, but would have my reps start by doing follow-up. These accounts liked working with me, so I was careful not to hand over each one until I knew the sales rep was ready and the company liked and trusted him or her.

After a year, I felt my salespeople were ready to take full responsibility, so I turned them loose—a little nervously, perhaps. Did it work? Did it ever!

Within eighteen months, sales at my major account had shot up from $7 million (me alone) to $13 million—none of it from me. Newly liberated, I decided to hold off selling the company for a couple of years because it was growing so much faster. For the first time, I was free to focus on the business in a big way, and when I finally did sell, the price had gone up considerably.

WORKSHEET 13A

Succession Plan Worksheet

Complete this worksheet as a guide to creating your succession plan.

1. Name your succession team.
   Department heads:
   Operations ____________________
   ____
   ____
   Sales ____________________
   Finance/accounting ____________________
   Human resources (HR) ____________________
   IT ____________________
   Business attorney ____________________
   Estate attorney ____________________

2. Department heads create process plans describing the different tasks they are responsible for, step-by-step. Provide each department head with a template (Worksheet 13B) so all process plans follow the same format. This will make things easier to follow.

3. Collect and create the process plans to form a user's guide/succession document.
   Create a hard copy and an electronic version.

4. Create *two* organization charts: One current, the other without you in the picture.

WORKSHEET 13A

Succession Plan Worksheet (Cont.)

5. Review ownership operating agreements. (Not necessary if you are a sole owner, but you'll need to develop the succession plan and get legal advice on how best to secure your wishes with respect to the business.)

Do you have an operating agreement? _______ If not, get one signed!

Consider each partner. Partner A might have only a financial stake, in which case you would probably recommend a buyout, whereas Partner B might have a key role in running operations, so you might opt for his stock to pass to his family. Remember that you can do what you like if all are in agreement, so there is no "right" answer here—only what's right for you and your partners.

What happens to their equity in the company?

	Partner A	Partner B
Buyout: What formula?	______________________	______________________

6. As part of your sales director's or manager's succession role, identify the relevant customers, then develop a plan to cover the accounts should a crisis occur with the individual currently working with the customer. Include the following information for all customers that are material in size through either sales or volume. Use a separate sheet for each customer.

Customer name ______________________

Current sales rep ______________________

Succession/crisis plan sales ______________________

____

____

Current customer service rep ______________________

Crisis plan customer service ______________________

____

7. Include replacing key management or other personnel. Who would step in and pick up the slack in a crisis, and how? Include people and processes, plus any other positions not listed here but crucial to your business.

Top sales reps:

Rep 1 ______________________

Rep 2 ______________________

Rep 3 ______________________

Office manager ______________________

Vice president of operations ______________________

____

Other (1) ______________________

____

Other (2) ______________________

____

WORKSHEET 13B

Process Plans (Department Head Template)

Department ____________________

Process development person ____________________

List your major tasks and the processes used to complete them.
Use a separate sheet for each task.

Task ____________________

Process used ____________________

Process map or chain

Key employees for this task

Key suppliers used in process ____________________

How would you streamline the process to make it more efficient?
Write a description or draw another process chain to illustrate your recommendation.

PART FOUR

Five Killer Mistakes

...

CHAPTER FOURTEEN
The "Yak Yak" Factor
Page 155

CHAPTER FIFTEEN
Invisibility
Page 161

CHAPTER SIXTEEN
The "Yee Haw!" Factor
Page 169

CHAPTER SEVENTEEN
Deal Fatigue
Page 175

CHAPTER EIGHTEEN
The Sudden Stop
Page 183

CHAPTER NINETEEN
The Last Word
Page 189

CHAPTER 14

The "Yak Yak" Factor

I LIKE TO WATCH THOSE CIRCUS PERFORMERS whose feats of dexterity and coordination leave everybody gasping with amazement: The horseback rider charging around the ring astride two white steeds, the plate spinner overseeing a priceless collection of dinnerware atop impossibly long sticks, the juggler keeping the air full of eggs, bowling pins, and chain saws all at the same time.

I can relate to this stuff, because I've become a bit of a juggler myself. I've started, run, and sold quite a few businesses, often more than one at a time. When it really got complicated was when I was not only running the business but dealing with several prospective buyers simultaneously, not to mention all the lawyers, accountants, and advisers involved in various aspects of the sale. It's a lot like spinning plates on sticks—only it's balancing jobs and money, and the stakes are a lot higher than a few dishes.

As you'll see, in this multiple role as chief business manager, company leader, and the top sales rep for the company as a whole, you can drop the ball in any of several critical areas, and all you can do is stand there and watch as the bowling pins and chainsaws come buzzing and bouncing down around you.

What follows will help you avoid dropping your business in mid-handoff.

Loose Lips Sink Ships

The first thing to remember is that a deal isn't a deal until the papers are signed and the money is in the bank. Before that happens, there are a million ways to mess it up. One of the easiest is to talk too much. It happens a lot. I call it the "Yak Yak" Factor.

With such big news on the horizon, some business owners give in to the urge to share the big secret with at least a few key people in the company. When they do, they forget a cardinal rule of leadership: If you don't want *all* of your employees to know something, don't tell *any* of them. Once a secret is told to one other person, it is no longer a secret.

It's a bad idea at this stage of the process, before anything has been decided, before the negotiations are even started, even to hint about things that may or may not happen. If you're inclined to share your thinking on important decisions with one or two of your favorite people, you can be sure that news this big—"You're selling the company!?"—will spread like a bad rash. Worse, it will mutate as it spreads. "I got it straight from HR that they're cutting seventy-five positions." "I heard they're shutting down this branch and splitting us up between Spokane and Texarkana." You haven't even received a firm offer, and already people's lives are in turmoil. They're worried about things that, in the end, are not all that likely to happen.

If you don't want *all* of your employees to know something, don't tell *any* of them.

Owners often rationalize such loose-lipped behavior by telling themselves or others that they believe in being open with their employees, or that they value their employees' opinions, and don't want to hold anything back. Yes, employees have a right to know about a decision that will affect them, but until that decision begins to take shape, loose talk is dangerous. Uncertainty leads to anxiety, lack of focus, and lower productivity, all of which hurt both the company and the people who run it.

It's wise to communicate well with your employees, especially your top management team, but sometimes we need to protect them from their own wild speculations and the emotional turmoil that comes from uncertainty. As much as you yearn to brag, to unburden yourself, to share your joy, you must not do it until you can control the effect. That's the price of leadership.

A Word to the Unwise

Andrea Fowler owned the Fowler Group, a small business consulting firm specializing in marketing. Andrea was approached by one of her competitors about selling her twelve-person company. The sale made sense; the companies specialized in different, sometimes unique and complementary services and had different client bases.

Andrea was excited. She was flattered that someone might want to buy the business she had spent years creating and building, and she was bursting at the seams to share the wonderful news with somebody. She chose Bill, president of operations and her closest confidante.

Andrea told him she was thinking of selling the company and wanted to know what he thought. Bill was taken aback. She had never before even hinted that she might want to sell out. He immediately had a number of questions:

- What will happen to our sales force?
- Will the compensation structure change?
- Will there be operational layoffs?
- We compete against these guys pretty fiercely; how can we work with them?
- What are you planning to do after you sell the company?

Andrea's answer to all five questions: "I don't know."

Bill left Andrea's office feeling blindsided and on shaky ground. Over the next two weeks, here's what happened:

- The entire organization was paralyzed; everyone was convinced he was going to lose his job.
- Work came to a virtual standstill.
- "The sellout" was the only thing anyone talked about.
- Employees began jockeying for position in the anticipated new organization.
- The company's largest client called Andrea to ask why she hadn't mentioned that she was selling her business.
- Two key employees quit and hired on at other companies; they told Andrea they couldn't wait around to find out if they could keep their jobs.

What eventually happened was typical. Not only did the prospect lose interest, but after thinking about it, Andrea herself decided she wasn't ready to sell. The business took a step backward; Andrea had to do a lot of fence-mending with employees, customers, and vendors. It was a rolling, unnecessary two-week disaster.

The Monkey Wrench Factor

When employers share sensitive information or speculation with employees, often it's not because they want to hear opinions or feedback, but because they are just bursting to tell someone the good news. They may think they're doing the right thing, "just being open with my employees," but this may be nothing more than a huge rationalization, and they're probably doing more harm than good. Here are a few examples of what can happen when word spreads about the potential sale of a company.

Crazy time. You'll be amazed at how some people act when money is involved. They think they're in for a windfall, or that they might not get their share. Either way, they go nuts—especially the employees who have been with you the longest and who you think are the most loyal. To delay this effect as long as possible, keep your lip zipped.

What happens to me? Most employees think that when a company gets sold, people get fired. In many cases this is true. Naturally, their first concern is about what happens to them after the deal goes through. Your future is looking great, theirs is a crapshoot. If you can't realistically explain to them what's going to happen and how to deal with it, springing a possible sale on them will only make them feel their time is limited.

Lack of focus. People working for you have their own dreams and aspirations. Having a job they can count on helps them feel secure and keeps them focused on their work; hearing that you might sell the company can burst their bubble in a hurry. This is the last thing you need when they should be concentrating on the business and making it look good to the prospective buyer.

Rivalry. At every level of the organization, inside information is power, and power signifies status. If you favor some employees with hot news, others will feel you don't consider them important or value their opinion. They feel left in the dark, out of control of their own careers. This translates into resentment, bad morale, and falling productivity. Even if the sale doesn't go through, the resentment and rivalry that is created may never go away.

Snoop City. Some of your employees like the power of being the information gatekeepers; they like to be the people other employees come to for information. When they get wind of really big news like a possible sale and new owners, they dig around to get the straight skinny. Inevitably, they get a lot of misinformation mixed in with the facts. This leads to false rumors, confusion, uncertainty, insecurity, anxiety, and lost productivity.

Talk of the town. If you are in the early stages of considering an offer, ask your potential buyer not to divulge any information or speculate out loud with his staff, other than on a strict need-to-know basis. The business world is like a small town; everybody knows somebody and people talk. If someone in your prospect's company begins shooting off his mouth, wild talk will quickly spread throughout your company, and a doubly inaccurate rumor from an outside source can be doubly destructive.

Stay alert for rumors floating around, especially the ones that get the facts wrong or are most likely to be disruptive. Be ready to spill the beans early if it appears that doing so would help decrease the uncertainty and keep morale high. Once the word is out, don't let bad information take control of your business.

KEEP YOUR DEALINGS CLOSE TO THE VEST

- *Don't talk about the deal on the telephone in front of other people*
- *Resist the urge to tell even your most trusted company confidante*
- *Put a fax machine in your office or another secluded space*
- *Discourage potential buyers from coming to your offices*
- *Hold meetings at your attorney's or the buyer's offices*
- *Never leave important documents lying around on your desk*
- *Lock your office at night*
- *Try to feign normalcy even as you're feeling stressed*

The highs and lows that come with considering a buyout deal are tough for you as an owner to handle by yourself. You can rely on your family, of course, but you really want to confide in your best employees, ask their advice, get their reactions to your ideas, and generally express your anxiety and your excitement. But you can't do it. Hey, that's why you get the big bucks. It's lonely at the top.

Time for the News

Preparing for the sale of your company is likely to be a difficult time for your people, so until you're pretty sure it's going to happen, it's better to keep quiet. There's no point in unnecessarily alarming your employees, and you don't want the embarrassment of having to explain to friends, family, or even the butcher down the street, why the deal didn't go through.

Keep in mind that most potential buyouts fall through—in my experience, about 70 percent. If your deal is among the 30 percent that progress to a firm offer, everyone in your company will be affected and share in the knowledge. You will have plenty of information to communicate to everyone once you've begun serious negotiations; until that time, zip it.

Keep a Tight Ship

One time, during the sale of a company, I left a sheet of paper on my desk that listed the stock options I'd proposed issuing to each of my top people. An employee spotted the list and word quickly spread around the office. I was immediately put on the defensive, having to explain why Person A would get more options than Person B. One key employee even threatened to quit. A benevolent gesture on my part came back to haunt me, all because I was careless enough to leave the sheet on my desk and my door open.

So be sure not to leave documents lying around in fax machines or on top of your desk. Lock important documents away every evening before you leave for home, and shut your door when you leave your office during the day. The reason is not necessarily that you don't trust your employees, but that you never want to put them in a position where they have to pretend they haven't seen sensitive information.

CHAPTER 15

Invisibility

A GOOD LEADER KNOWS WHEN TO DELEGATE responsibility and when to handle things himself. You can trust others to handle duties that are routine, well designed, trainable, and noncritical—that is, responsibilities for which the person assigned is fully qualified or, if not, in which a mistake won't mean instant disaster. You don't give the night shift at the reactor to an all-new crew. You don't let Junior land the airliner while you're catching forty winks.

Often it's the boring stuff you assign to a subordinate while you're out front taking care of strategy and nonroutine events like fighting off alligators or being interviewed on *Larry King Live*. So it wouldn't seem as though negotiating the maze of selling your company would be something you could delegate.

And yet it happens—more often than you might imagine.

One reason it happens is that many business owners feel outside their comfort zone because they have little or no experience selling a business. It seems safer, not to mention easier, to turn over the details to specialists. These include lawyers, who communicate with the buyer's lawyers and ensure that the deal meets all legal requirements; accountants, who present financial information and certify the spreadsheets for your business and the buyer's; your own managers, who can explain the structure and operation of your business to the buyer from the perspective of their own roles; and assorted advisers, brokers, and specialists.

And the truth is, once you get over the first flush of excitement about getting an offer and negotiating a price with lots of zeroes in it, dotting the i's and crossing the t's can seem pretty dull—stuff for your well-paid accountants and lawyers to do.

The danger is that once the deal seems to be a sure thing, the seller sometimes not only turns over the details to others, but also checks out of the process.

It's okay to yield the floor to your representatives in their specific areas of expertise because, after all, they are there to represent you and your interests and to help you make decisions. They provide information so *you* can make the call. However—and this is crucial—do not just turn things over to others and expect it all to work out. Remember: You will be the one living with the outcome.

Vanishing Act

Maria Alvarez was the founder and owner of Alvarez Marketing Group (AMG). She had spent ten years growing her business into one of the leading agencies targeting the Hispanic marketplace, building a solid customer base of top-tier clients and carving a competitive niche in the ultracompetitive world of marketing and advertising agencies. Alvarez Marketing aligned itself with best-in-class partners to provide their clients with a full-service approach to the Hispanic market that included activities such as database management, general advertising, direct marketing, event marketing, and electronic marketing.

Do not just turn things over to others and expect it all to work out. Remember: You will be the one living with the outcome.

AMG was a good-sized family business, with sales around $3 million and profits of $500,000. Maria knew that the marketing industry was consolidating and that three or four of the really big mainstream agencies in the space were trying to gobble up all the best small specialty agencies, especially those with nice profit margins and solid customer bases. She knew that the clients of these large marketing firms were demanding more capabilities from them and thought that having Hispanic marketing capabilities would be a big advantage to them. So Maria figured it was time to take a look and even consider selling.

She had been approached before but hadn't pursued a sale because she didn't think the time was right. Now things were different. Not only was the industry looking for her type of business, but Maria was ready to move her business onto a larger stage and see some rapid growth. A large company's financial clout, contacts, and capability would make that possible. She also wouldn't mind the security of having cash in her pocket for all her years of hard work.

One of these large companies contacted Maria about buying AMG. She knew it was a solid organization, well respected in the marketing and advertising community. She responded smartly: She said she might be interested, but that AMG was doing great and that she expected it to grow substantially over the next few years. The potential buyer was intrigued and wanted to talk more, so Maria agreed to a meeting. They discussed business philosophy, and the company gave her the standard purchaser pitch—all the reasons she should sell and how wonderful it would be for her in the new organization.

Maria returned from her meeting pumped up about her company's prospects. Being a smart business owner, she wondered: Would anyone else be interested? She hired a firm to represent her and discreetly test the waters. Three more prospects were identified, and the bidding war was off and running.

For the next eight weeks, Maria played a lead role, meeting frequently with each of the prospective buyers with an eye to finding the perfect home for her company. She reached an agreement on general terms with the company that had first contacted her and accepted an offer sheet with a sell price of $2.5 million. She thought the offer was perfect: She would take on a larger role within the parent company, and AMG would be the platform for other acquisitions the parent company would make.

As the diligence and sell process continued, Maria spent more and more time thinking about her new role and how she would grow AMG with the backing of the new organization. She had put together a team consisting of a couple of her senior managers, her finance director, an attorney, and the representative she had previously hired. This team handled the details of the diligence process. Maria turned most of her attention back to the business, occasionally working out a strategy that would allow her to hit the ground running. She knew she had a great and loyal team, so she decided to stay out of their way and let them handle this part of the sale.

It was about 8:00 A.M. and Maria was in her office when she got the call: The buyer was pulling out! But why? Two reasons, they said. They didn't feel that the management team was on the same page as the owner with respect to growing the business, and they felt that they might inherit recent customer problems.

Over the course of three weeks, the deal had disintegrated. The reason: Maria wasn't there to steer the bus and never saw it heading for the cliff. In her absence, here's what happened.

In an effort to be viewed in a positive light by their prospective new boss, her current employees jockeyed for position: They talked about the company's problems and boasted of how they would fix them. Every business has problems, of course, but letting employees talk about them at this stage raised doubts about the business in the buyer's mind.

Maria had presented her company's expectations at her initial meetings and outlined AMG's plan for growth, including expansion into new services and other big ideas. This included a lot of information she hadn't yet told her employees. Later, when the buyer had questions, Maria wasn't around to answer them; her normally excellent and well-spoken employees appeared incompetent, and the bad information they provided caused more doubts. The same was true of information about AMG's clients. Had Maria still been in the game at this point, she could easily have squelched these issues. By the time she learned about them, it was too late.

The problems didn't end with the demise of the original offer. The rumor mill had already cranked up. This made it impossible to get any meaningful price at all, at least for the present—and the economics might never again be so favorable.

Maria was a fast learner; she didn't make the same mistakes eighteen months later when entertaining an offer from a different buyer. In the meantime, however, the business had a little hiccup, so it fetched only $1.5 million the second time around.

Read the Fine Print

If you've ever seen documents for the acquisition of a company, you know just how absurdly long they are—like the New York City Yellow Pages, except filled with a mountain of details covering every conceivable fact, number, stipulation, whereas and wherefore. It takes a supreme effort of will to pore through them. Many of us simply put our faith in the capable hands of our attorneys and let them deal with all that "lawyer stuff."

That's what Maggie Wilcox did when she sold her online dating service. Many aspects of her business figured into the valuation, such as the marketing database that included profiles and opt-in approvals of registered customers. Trying to keep the business running with one hand (to optimize the sell price) and going through due diligence with the other, she was swamped.

Many of us simply put our faith in the capable hands of our attorneys and let them deal with all that "lawyer stuff."

Finally she and the lawyer agreed on a price of $5.3 million. Maggie was excited, anxious to close the deal so she could collect her millions. In order to continue running the business, though, she decided to have her attorney handle the details of the contract work. Her only real concern was to shore up the sell price and leave her business in good shape for the new owners.

Papers were signed. Everything seemed great. Then it was time to receive the money. Maggie checked her bank account every day

The Basket

When a company is sold, the deal often includes assurances by the seller that certain things will happen: A patent will be granted, a major new customer contract will come in, and the like. These representations and warranties—the "basket"—are often covered by money held back until they are fulfilled. The amount held back, as well as the time frame of the basket, becomes part of the negotiation and is written into the contract. The basket can range from zero to the entire amount of the sell price.

for the completion of the $5.3 million wire. On Tuesday she looked, and there it was—$2.3 million?!

Once past her initial panic, Maggie called the buyer to ask about the rest of the money. This is when she heard that her actual cash payment terms would hold back $3 million to be paid twelve months from the closing date. Why? Because, according to the contract Maggie had signed, she had to leave $3 million in escrow to cover the "basket"—representations and warranties that she had made about the business during the sell process. More to the point, the buyer was buying data, technology, and processes that Maggie had lauded as best in class for her company. She had promoted a couple of lucrative contracts that were scheduled to close within the upcoming year; she had made the representation and received valuation for these items even though they hadn't yet been signed.

Unfortunately for Maggie, she was so intent on getting the deal done but so removed from the negotiations that she didn't review any of the documents, and since reps and warranties are pretty standard, everyone, including her attorney, incorrectly assumed that she knew about them and would have looked for them. But Maggie would rather have had her fingers slammed in a car door than spend time reading thick legal documents, so she had just sat back and let others decide her fate.

After a few painful days of push-and-pull, Maggie relented and settled for the $2.3 million at close and $3 million one year later. Everything worked out for Maggie in the long run—she got her $5.3 million—but she got lucky. Maggie's database might not have lived up to the buyer's expectations—one of her large customers might have flown the coop and the buyer could have felt misled. In fact, any one of a hundred things could have happened to cause the buyer to dip into that $3 million pot. The task is to make sure this doesn't happen to you. Any one of a hundred things could have happened to cause the buyer to dip into that $3 million pot.

What to Do

I'm like Maggie. I hate, *really* hate, looking at legal documents. They are long and boring, and they're in a language I don't understand, so what's the point? Well, Steve, the point is that if you don't find out what the papers say before you sign them, you may be in for a surprise—and as any lawyer can tell you, *surprise* is a legal term that means "Gotcha!"

Suppose you've accepted an offer of $5 million for your company and that as one term of the sale, you've agreed to step away from the business and have no further part in running it. Suppose that you've also unknowingly agreed to representations and warranties totaling $5 million. Now your entire purchase price is at risk. If your company, which is no longer under your control, materially breaches the reps and warranties clause of the agreement, you may be standing on the street with your pockets hanging out. All because you didn't bother to understand what you were agreeing to. (This is an extreme example. Normally, any good attorney will make sure you fully understand the deal points, but in Maggie's case this didn't quite happen. Bottom line: Be prudent and check everything.)

As any lawyer can tell you, *surprise* is a legal term that means "Gotcha!"

So you have to bite the bullet and read the fine print. However, there's an easy way to handle the problem of legalese-induced coma. It's really pretty simple, and not all that expensive. When I'm preparing to sell a company, I have my attorney walk me through the documents page by page, translating them into English as we go: purchase agreement, employment agreement, any other crucial documents. This takes maybe a couple of hours, so the legal fees aren't that bad. More important, I understand the important details: pric-

Limit Your Exposure

I believe in keeping the representations and warranties tightly defined—that is, don't put in a lot of conditions that are subject to interpretation and can be contested. A properly conducted due diligence protects the buyer; make the reps and warranties as narrow and favorable to yourself as you can. However, if you make claims in order to get a higher price, such as "I'm sure I'm going to get this additional piece of business," expect to be asked to put your money where your mouth is. You may well be asked to make a warranty to that representation, which can mean returning money to the buyer or settling for a lower sell price if you don't make good on it. If you do make such statements, try to remain steadfast and avoid guaranteeing them in your basket.

ing formulas that determine the ultimate sell price, representations and warranties, the details of my new employment contract, what happens to my employees' jobs, and anything else I or the seller has introduced as a condition of the sale.

Three Reasons to Stay in the Game

This aspect of selling your business—the fine print—is probably the least fun. It means reading boring documents, discussions regarding details of the transaction, lots of hours listening to experts debate the finer points of the deal. Nowhere near as much fun as starting a business, making that first big-bucks deal, or taking your family sailing on your brand-new yacht. But when it comes down to the point of sale, it's important that you stay fully engaged in the process. Why? Three reasons:

1. **No one knows the business like you.** Your managers should know their particular areas well, perhaps better than you, but you and you alone will have the "view from ten thousand feet," the overall picture of the business. This is what the buyer will assume, and this is why you need to be the quarterback for the sale. Your presence and readiness to explain any aspect of your business will help make the buyer comfortable with the sale.

2. **You must troubleshoot.** The buyer will probably have a team of people running his diligence process—the bigger the deal, the more people—all asking questions about your business. Of course, you will have your own people helping you, but your ability to answer questions immediately, in person, and in a consistent manner will have a great impact. It will also show your managers how to handle questions when you're not around.

3. **You have the most to gain.** Other people in your company have their own dreams and ambitions, and the sale of your company probably isn't one of them. They may be helpful and sympathetic, but with so many uncertainties in their own future, they're not likely to break their backs to maximize the sell price. You're probably the big winner, whether it's by getting the lion's share of the cash, landing a good job in the new company, or having the freedom to walk away rich. It's not that your people wish you harm; it's just human not to put forth their best effort when somebody else gets the biggest payout. Completing a sale is hard, stressful, and a roller coaster of emotion. It's unfair to expect others to take the ride for you.

CHAPTER 16

The "Yee Haw!" Factor

HERE'S HOW IT GOES: You've got a prospective buyer for your company, and you're spending a lot of your time working on the deal. This means you're not only running the business, you're thinking about a lot of other things at the same time. Maybe it's that new company you're going to start that you think will take off and grow into something big. Maybe it's the round-the-world cruise you and your spouse are planning to take as soon as the money is in the bank. Or maybe it's just the fun and novelty of working on the sale, a goal you've had ever since you started your business.

Things start to get complicated. A few customers get wind of the deal and complain that they aren't being kept in the loop; they're concerned about their own business and whether you'll be able or available to serve them down the road. Rumors fly; a couple of key employees get nervous and find jobs elsewhere. Shipments don't arrive on time; quality slips.

Normally, you would jump in with both feet, call a few dozen people, take a few trips, tackle the challenges, and enjoy the satisfaction of finessing such problems into oblivion. But these days your mind is elsewhere. Rather than thinking about cash flow, current customers, and growth projections, you find yourself daydreaming about extreme skiing, African safaris, and finally being able to attend your daughter's violin recitals. You've mentally checked out and left no forwarding address.

At some point in the process of selling your business, you're going to have to deal with the "Yee Haw!" Factor—the psychological state that occurs when, in your mind, you've switched from being the owner of your business to being the seller and you're blinded by big dollar signs. The problem is that the sale hasn't been completed. This makes you vulnerable. Why? Because if you're thinking about all the great times you're going to have as soon as you sell the business, your mind is not on the business or the deal and you're likely to miss important details in both—and because psychologically, you're so committed to the sale that you're ready to give a little to make sure the deal goes through.

"Yee Haw!" Factor—the psychological state that occurs when, in your mind, you've switched from being the owner of your business to being the seller and you're blinded by big dollar signs.

As a buyer of businesses, I would keep an eye out for the "Yee Haw!" Factor in my counterpart. Typically it would show up as a pulling away from the business and letting it drift a bit out of control. Once I saw signs of the Yee Haws, I knew I could get better terms than what was on the table. Sure, it would bother me that the owner's Yee Haw coma caused his business to take a temporary hit, but I knew that the terms were about to get more favorable for me.

Here are three tips to help you fight off the Yee Haws:

Overfill your time. Immerse yourself in your current work and not just the task of selling your business. You'll have little time for anything else, including daydreaming. Think of it this way: If the deal goes through, you'll be leaving the business in great shape. If you have an earn-out structure (see chapter 7, "Payout Structure and Currency"), you'll be better positioned to collect a greater amount. And if the deal doesn't go through, your business won't be sufferin' the broken-deal blues, it'll be cookin' along better than ever.

Talk to yourself. Over 70 percent of proposed deals fall through, many at the last minute. That means the odds are greater than one chance out of two that your deal will not be completed. Write this down and leave it where you'll see it every day. Something as simple as "Nothing's done yet" or "Stay focused" will do just fine. I usually put it on small display in my home office, where I work at night, as a gentle reminder to keep my foot on the accelerator.

Imagine the buyer leaving tomorrow. Will your business be in shambles or can you easily pick up the pieces? You need to keep this in the back of your mind, because when it happens, it happens fast.

Hello, Anybody Home?

Segment Design, a small but highly creative interior design firm, was in negotiations with The Berkeley Group, a large roll-up company that already owned several other design firms. Berkeley was growing through acquisitions, and Mary Beth Moore, Segment Design's president, saw Berkeley as a logical home for her design firm. She was ready to sell and had been for several years. She had spent the past fifteen years working hard to build her firm into a successful niche player and was really looking forward to some time for herself.

Berkeley offered Mary Beth an earn-out deal that would pay her three times her firm's average profits for the next three years—in other words, the sum of her next three years' profits. By her own projections, this could amount to $3.6 million, maybe even more if she could land a couple more large clients. This was huge money to Mary Beth; it would let her do all of the things she'd been dreaming about.

The negotiations continued, as did the diligence process. After five weeks of intense work, long hours, and numerous sacrifices, it looked like things were finally moving toward closure. About time, thought Mary Beth. She knew she was spread too thin. She also knew that the proposed earn-out structure and future riches would be a reality only if she could deliver profits to the future owner, and the time she was spending on this deal was cutting into those profits. She was having to neglect her loyal customers, and their irritation was showing.

Mary Beth had been talking to the buyer several times a day, but now she was happy because it had been two days since their last discussion, and she had been able to reconnect with her clients. As she began to smooth things out, she found that they were more upset and feeling more neglected than she had imagined. At least it wouldn't be in vain, she thought, because after all, she was about to sign a huge exit deal.

Another day went by with no word from the prospective buyer. Mary Beth wanted to wrap things up quickly, but when she called the prospect, she got a voice mail. This made her nervous. She called again and left an urgent-sounding voice mail asking the prospect to call her as soon as possible.

The next day, when she checked her own voice mail, she got the bad news. Berkeley was sorry, but it was no longer interested in purchasing her firm; Segment Design was a wonderful company, and they thought she was terrific, but they had funding problems with another project and wouldn't have the money to pay for Segment.

Mary Beth was stunned. All that time and effort, the lost opportunity, the angry clients, and upset employees—all for nothing. The normally reserved Mary Beth left a return voice-mail message in a special locker-room language, but after she had blown off some steam, she still had to deal with a business that was suffering and clients who were less than pleased with her. She and her team spent the next two months mending fences and saving accounts.

What happens? You're eager to start your new life of freedom, wealth, and leisure—but you're still the head of your business, and your business is still galloping along. It's like swapping horses in mid-gallop. It can be done—you've seen it at the circus—but if one horse is racing flat-out and the other one's cantering along, you're going to end up flat on your face. One of two outcomes is likely:

- The deal goes through and, as usually happens, you agree on an earn-out structure, but because you've been preoccupied, your business suffers and doesn't make as much profit, which means that you don't make nearly as much on the ultimate payout.
- The deal doesn't go through and now you have a problem. Your business is suffering, your employees are upset, and you're depressed because your dream has to wait a bit longer. Depending on the situation, some businesses never fully recover from this neglect.

How to Stay in the Saddle

In my experience, staying in full control of your business while negotiating the maze of preparing for acquisition is a job that can be done but requires mental preparation. Here are some of the things you can do to set your mind right:

Plan for the sale. Get your business in shape before you even start the sell process. Having simple documents ready, such as historical financials, an organizational chart, a list of business processes and brands, growth strategies, and projections, will cut down the freak-out factor and midnight-oil burning later on when you are asked for these items. (See chapter 3, "Prepare Your Company," for more.)

Be prepared to put the sale on hold. Don't become so focused on the sale that you let your current business suffer. For the health of your company and of your payout, make sure your business is operating at maximum efficiency when the time comes to sign the papers.

One Step Back, One Million Steps Forward

I received an offer for my first business, with a purchase price based on a multiple of earnings. At the time, I didn't have a lot of depth in my company, so in addition to running the business, I was bringing in almost 90 percent of the sales myself. I knew that if I were to try to hand over the keys to my company during my customer's peak budget process, the business and ultimately the purchase price would suffer.

The offer was terrific. It would have meant instant wealth and leisure. I was mightily tempted. Nevertheless, I told the buyer the timing was wrong and I needed to focus on the business for a while, but that I'd love to pick up the offer in a few months, after the budget cycle was over. This was a risky move. The buyer might find another company in my space, hit a profit snag, or just lose interest. So when I say put the process on hold, I don't say it lightly.

The risk paid off. Ultimately the move netted me many millions more. It allowed me to leave a solid business, and I got the respect of the buyer, who had firsthand evidence that I really cared about the business and would be a valuable asset to them post acquisition. This was important to me. I was young and had no intention of leaving the business world. I was just getting started.

Be conscious of your operations. Don't tie up your key personnel in the sell process when they may need to work on the business. You don't want to hobble the company just as it's being sold. Make these key employees available to meet the prospective buyer on *your* terms; this way, you can manage their time away from the business. Your buyer will appreciate your commitment to your company and to making sure that it doesn't have a hiccup. Remember, the buyer is going to end up with the business after the sale, and who wouldn't want a business in great shape? It's a lot like buying a house: First you inspect it, then you buy it. If things start going wrong after you move in, you may suspect you were sold a lemon, but you're stuck with it. It's the same with a business.

Add short-term incentives. Short-term incentives may be just the thing to keep everyone's attention focused. Mini-sales contests and bonus programs to control costs are two of the many ways you can keep people's minds from wandering and reward profit-driving activities. The cost of the small prizes for these quickies should be more than made up for by the higher dollar your company will command at the gavel—especially if the purchase price is based on a multiple of profit.

CHAPTER 17

Deal Fatigue

IN SIX YEARS PHILLIP JONES HAD TRANSFORMED TechSave, his home-based IT data storage start-up, into a major business with more than ten employees in nice offices and revenues over $7 million. He was so good at managing costs that he had realized a net profit of $2.1 million—that's 30 percent!

Phil was making great money, but after eight years of working seven days a week, twelve hours a day, he was ready to sell TechSave and get out of the fast lane for a while. He set his target date for a year down the road.

Being a savvy deal maker, he began positioning his business for sale by doing all the right things. First he set out to make himself superfluous; he trained more people and installed processes that would make the business less dependent on him. He put together a business sell team, created an offering memorandum, made a killer business-overview presentation, organized solid audited financial statements, worked with his team to pitch prospects and assess their offers, and set the valuation at $8.6 million. He even set up a data room complete with the information prospective buyers would need to complete their diligence on the company.

Phil did all this while continuing to run the company as before. This bumped his workload from twelve to sixteen hours a day—crazy hours, but he wanted to be sure there weren't any speed bumps along the way to the sale. He was covering the downside, too: If the sale fell through, he wanted to be sure TechSave wouldn't be badly damaged.

Fourteen months later Phil was still going at it. He'd found a buyer and agreed to terms for a purchase price of $8.3 million (only $300,000 off his original valuation), and the deal was moving ahead. Then it came time for the diligence phase, where the potential buyer got to look into the guts of the business.

Over the next six weeks, the two sides went back and forth on a number of issues. Phillip and his team spent hours educating the potential buyer on the details of the business. They dealt with many questions and concerns, some of which led to adjustments in valuation, payoff terms, and post-close representations and warranties. The buyer was continually asking for more and more information and kept coming up with reasons for the amount of the sale to be lowered, while Phil and his team lobbied for an increase in valuation and sell price, citing the continued successes of the business year and the strategic fit of TechSave in the buyer's growth strategy. This exchange went on and on, and over the next several weeks, the buyer asked for more and more concessions.

After nearly a year and half of hard work, handling most of the load himself, Phil was beyond stressed out; the buyer, with more people working on the deal, still had plenty of negotiating vigor. Time dragged on. Phil grew tired, emotionally drained, even depressed. He sometimes found himself wondering if the deal would ever close.

For more than a year, Phil had been dreaming of how life would be after he sold TechSave: Trips to exotic destinations, buying his parents a new home, the freedom of knowing he would never *have* to work again. He was tired of the deal dragging on, anxious to get on with his new life—and vulnerable.

Here's what happened: He found himself relenting on more and more of the buyer's demands. He had little energy left to argue even the bigger issues. He had deal fatigue.

A typical business sale negotiation includes one final push by the buyer to reduce the price by bringing up negative findings from the diligence process. In TechSave's case, the buyer had doubts about some of the technology the company owned and some of the contracts it had signed.

As tireless a worker as Phil was, he finally ran out of steam. His patience was exhausted. He wanted to get his money and get out. He was ready to agree to anything to make this happen. So he threw in the towel. Yes, he would lower the price.

He ended up selling for $6.9 million, a substantial drop from the initial offer. Although we won't be holding any charity fund-raisers for Phil, the fact is that he suffered from a condition that cost him $1.4 million—deal fatigue.

Sick of the Whole Thing

It might seem strange to you that Phil would feel this way—so tired of the whole selling thing that he would essentially cut his own throat. After all, he was making great money, his business was kicking butt, and like most entrepreneurs, he loved this kind of work. Truth is, though, it happens a lot more often than you'd expect—and an experienced buyer might even attempt to push a seller into this state.

It's the combined effects of total commitment, the effort given, the sheer amount of work involved, the lack of sleep, the roller-coaster emotions, and the tantalizing future that seems to stay just out of reach. It all comes together in the great big freeway pileup known as deal fatigue.

IF YOU WANT TO BE ANALYTICAL ABOUT IT, DEAL FATIGUE HAS FOUR MAIN COMPONENTS

- The sheer effort that must be committed to shaping a deal that will fly
- The emotional ups and downs of dealing with each day's good news or bad news
- The conflicts that arise between your wishes and the buyer's demands
- The time it takes, which often seems to stretch beyond your emotional horizon

It probably won't surprise you to know, however, that deal fatigue isn't limited to the seller. The same factors listed above apply to the buyer as well. Buyers often get stressed out and fed up with delays and, as a result, can end up paying too much for the business. The less experienced the buyer, the more likely the buyer is to succumb to deal fatigue.

Once the lawyer has been negotiating with you for a while, the

WHY YOU NEED TO MANAGE EVERY EMOTION

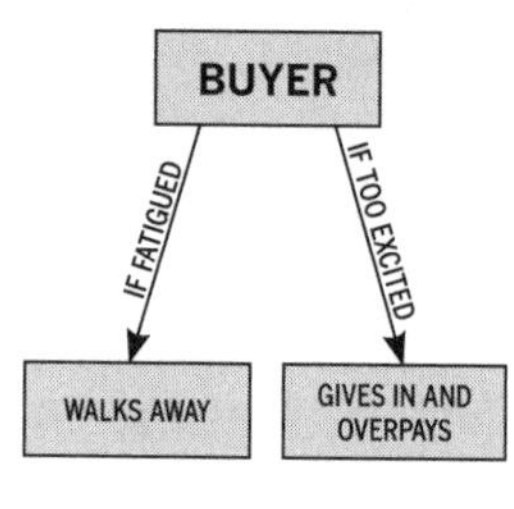

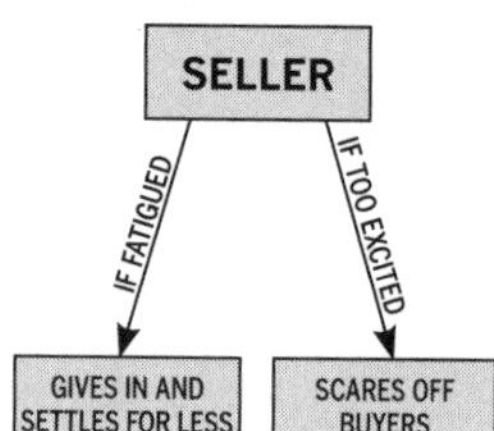

buyer may begin to feel vested in the sale. While you're daydreaming about the good times ahead after you sell the company and pocket your cash, it has started thinking ahead about all the wonderful things it can do with the company, the prestige of acquiring a new business identity and market, the competitive power it will have. Just like you, the buyer really wants the sale to happen.

But there's a twist. When sellers fall victim to deal fatigue, they're more likely to give in and settle for a lower price than to throw up their hands and walk away. Buyers are different; walking out is more likely than caving in. That is, as the seller you are typically more vested in the sale than the buyer.

Therefore, a good selling strategy for you would be to lead the buyer into feeling excited and optimistic about the deal, without pushing so hard that the buyer gets deal fatigue. If that happens, you may end up holding the bag and looking for another buyer.

Staving Off Deal Fatigue

Athletes know that a good workout leads to feelings of renewed vigor and well-being, not total exhaustion and fatigue. They get ready for exercise by stretching and flexing and through mental preparation. In the same way, you can prepare for a tough deal-making competition, and both the sprint and the distance events that it includes, by a bit of mental and managerial limbering up. Here are some issues to keep in mind as you prepare yourself for a tough but flexible, vigorous but self-preserving, sale negotiation:

Know what's coming. One of the most common causes of deal fatigue, but fortunately one of the easiest to overcome, is faulty time expectations—mainly, thinking that the process is further along than it actually is. It's like driving down an unfamiliar road without a map: You keep going and going, with no apparent end in sight. All you know is that you're tired of driving and want to get to your destination—*now!* About 98 percent of company sales follow a set process, which is difficult to circumvent. Knowing and feeling comfortable with the process will go far toward helping you stave off deal fatigue. Study the process. Know what's next and how long it will take, so that you can manage your time expectations. Reading this book will get you there.

Manage highs and lows. The buy-sell process is a bit of a roller coaster. To manage the peaks and the valleys, stand back and take a broader perspective. Use your knowledge of the process to see where the highs and lows are likely to occur. Consider your employees: What will they be anxious about? You already know which of your people will be the most troubled. Anticipate their issues and how you'll deal with them.

The Ten-Second Rule

Here's a technique that I often use successfully to smooth out the highs and lows of business life, and of life in general. Before you react to any news, pause for a full ten seconds. This may not sound like much time, but believe me, it can be an eternity. And when you're a leader and people around you are taking their cues from you, it can make a world of difference. Try it now; take any issue you're facing, look at your watch, and think for just ten seconds. You'll be amazed at how many ideas this will stir up—new perspectives, possible solutions, different strategies that you didn't even know your unconscious mind was considering. The ten-second hold also gives you time to figure out what's really happening and helps you avoid overreacting. Of course, simply looking at your watch, counting off ten, or freezing in place may send the wrong message or make the other person uncomfortable, so I recommend building the ten-second stall into another behavior to disguise it. For example, say, "Let me get back to you this afternoon," or "Meet me in my office in five minutes," or "Stay here, I'll be right back," and then excuse yourself for thirty seconds. This gives you time to think without being pressured for an immediate response. It will make your life easier, make you seem wiser, and keep you on an even keel.

Understand time vesting. Know that both parties want the deal to happen—otherwise they wouldn't be making the offer. Don't confuse tough negotiating with a rejection of your sale proposal or issue. As time goes on, both you and the buyer will become more and more vested in the sale; to encourage commitment, make sure the buyer spends as much time on the deal as possible. One way to do this is to get the buyer to work harder to get your agreement. I've mentioned this earlier in the book, but it bears repeating: Do some diligence of your own and ask why the buyer's organization is right for you. Ask to meet the managers or those who will be working with or on the business once it's acquired. Have them explain why you should sell to them instead of someone else. Focus on the strategic and business growth opportunities rather than economics, because growth is what is best for you and your employees and is probably what the buyer is really after anyway.

Take a mental break. Of course, you must keep managing your business, but don't push it. Here's another benefit of understanding the process: knowing there will be natural break times between some of the process steps. Let's say you're in a bit of a funk, working on yet another buyer request: another schedule of projections, another list of processes, whatever. Knowing that a break is just around the corner lets you suck it up a bit and do what needs to be done instead of making a half-baked effort. Back when I was in school and totally sick of studying, I would think ahead to the next holiday break or the next party, which usually wasn't too far down the road, and that would get me through the day. That's pretty much what I do when business gets me down—I go for a mental ramble. When you see there's nothing useful to be done, check out for a bit and go mindless. Watch a good movie, read a book—anything to give your mind a rest or a change of pace.

If you have to put the deal on hold for a while to focus on your business, do so.

Exercise. Selling a company will drain you just as much physically as mentally, so go for a run, work out, take a bike ride, or just take the dog for a walk, but make the time for some physical activity. It's good for your mind as well as your body. You'll see things more clearly. I can't count how many times I've figured out the solution to a problem while running. This includes the writing of this book; when I needed to explain a concept but was a little "locked," I'd go for a run, and almost invariably the solution would come to me at some point in the run.

Eat right. Now this is where I tell you, "Do as I say, not as I do," because I'm a junk-food junkie (I'm trying to get over it). My negotiating abilities suffer when I'm eating a lot of fatty food; I get sluggish and lethargic. Sweets do the same: momentary boost, quick crash. Stick with a balanced diet and get some sleep. In fact, combine the exercise and nutrition tips into a single regimen. Think of it as training for a big athletic event. You can't play if you're slow and lazy, mentally or physically. Training keeps you sharp. Your future and your dreams depend on it.

What if it doesn't work? Keep in mind that many deals fall through, for many reasons—so don't burn your bridges. If you have to put the deal on hold for a while to focus on your business, do so. Do everything necessary to make sure your business will continue should the deal go south.

Remain steadfast. Selling a business isn't for the squeamish. To do it successfully, you have to manage many agendas, personalities, and constituents. It's tough physically and mentally, but don't settle. Remember, you have something those other folks are very interested in buying—otherwise they wouldn't be across the table. Resolve to complete the deal on your own terms. If you can pull it off, you just might be set for life.

CHAPTER 18

The Sudden Stop

AFTER YEARS OF WORKING EIGHTEEN-HOUR DAYS and seven-day weeks, who hasn't had the urge to just walk away from it all? Wouldn't it be a relief to have no schedule, no appointments, no decisions to make, no problems to solve, nothing to do all day? Not necessarily.

For someone who has been totally involved in starting, growing, and running a business, getting out of the game suddenly can be like leaving a roller coaster on impulse—not a good idea. It's like what can happen when, with no planning whatsoever, a professional athlete retires at the top of his game.

I'll illustrate this point with the story of one business owner whose experience shows what can happen even when you know how to avoid this killer mistake. Let's call him Steve Kaplan.

After I sold one of my larger businesses, my home run sale, I decided to stay in the company for about four more years. I ran the profit and loss, and I flew around the globe buying and selling businesses. It was a great time, but I finally got tired of flying through the night across oceans to get home in time to coach my son's Little League game or make it to my daughter's dance recitals. It started

THINGS TO DO POST-SALE

- *Coach Little League*
- *Open an art gallery*
- *Begin a foundation*
- *Buy your parents a new home*
- *Take dance lessons*
- *Write a novel*
- *Learn a foreign language*
- *Travel around the world*
- *Spend more time with your family*
- *Start another business*

getting to me. I decided I'd rather be home with my family while my kids were young than to be doing all that traveling. If I sold my business, I could afford to do that and my time would be my own. I wrapped everything up and stepped away from the business. I was forty years old.

Even though I had planned for this day for about a year, I remember vividly my first day away from the business and the loss I felt as I went from the leader of a global organization, responsible for over sixteen hundred employees in more than a dozen countries, to having no employees and nothing but time on my hands—within the span of a single day. A bit of a shock.

However, I managed to avoid going into free fall, which is the killer mistake I speak of. Right before I sold the business, I got some of the best advice I've ever received. A person for whom I have a lot of respect counseled me to ponder the following question:

If and when you leave, what are you going to do after you've had your few days of rest?

It's a deceptively simple-sounding question, but as I thought about it, I began to see a lot of insight hidden in its corners.

After all the years I had spent building my business, I realized that the business had become a part of me. It was like raising a child: How could I ever walk away? You'd think that having the money, freedom, and financial security would be enough to say, "Hasta la vista, baby, it's off to the beach!" But I'll tell you what—most often that's not the case.

A Plan for Not Running a Business

Entrepreneurs are a special breed. We love our work, we love our companies, we love leading people toward meaningful goals. When we have this, we're happy, but if we wake up one day without it, poof! Instant depression. Many business owners close the sale, take the money, step back to catch their breath—then slide into a depression that ends only when they start another business.

Now, I'm not saying that this is a given and that every person who sells a business will fall into a funk, but it's more than just a possibility, and it's not all that uncommon. You say, "It'll never happen to me. I'll be more than happy doing nothing," but if you don't plan for the day when this event occurs, you can almost be sure that it *will* happen. If for several years most of every waking hour has been devoted to growing and running your business, part of your identity resides in that business, and if suddenly it's no longer there, it's a bit like having something amputated. Some people get through it, adapt, and thrive; others are never the same.

I'm a very positive person, and I typically think things through. I had planned my departure for over a year. I had lists of things to do, including writing books on the business success factors I wish I had known when I was starting out. This kept me busy. I also coached my son's sports teams, spent quality time with my daughter, and took minor roles in several other companies.

Yet even with all these things to keep me busy, I managed to slide into a persistent case of the blues. I missed the stage. I missed the travel, the pressure, the heartaches, the big wins, the big losses, and, yes, even the struggle. I missed being at the helm of a big undertaking, with hundreds, perhaps thousands, of people looking to me for leadership.

Because of this, I was less than a pleasure to deal with for a while, and being home full-time took quite an adjustment—for everyone. Eventually, though, I settled in, and within a few years, I was back doing what I loved best—building another business. Well, okay, it was a couple of businesses, but my main business was consulting and public speaking. I loved starting things, and I was beginning a whole new career: helping other businesses grow bigger, better, and faster. Now I can spend a lot of time at home and still play a meaningful role in the business, so life is good.

I've spoken with many business owners who have sold their companies, and they've had similar experiences. It was rough for a while, but I can hardly imagine how bad it would have been if I hadn't anticipated how hard it would be to make the transition from on-the-go business owner to unemployed man of leisure.

After the Sale

How can you prepare yourself to handle the letdown that goes with letting go of the business that has been your baby from infancy? It's not easy, but there are a number of actions you can take to stiffen your spine, ease your mind, and pave the way for a smoother transition before you exit stage left. Some may seem a bit odd to you, but I've found all of these tips extremely helpful:

You are an employee now! Acknowledge that you are no longer the owner of the business. You have a boss, and the final decisions probably aren't yours anymore or, if they are yours, are mandated by your acquirer. Get used to it. Accept the fact you have to detach yourself emotionally from the business.

Divest yourself. Whether your company is large or small, you need to organize it well enough to make yourself nonessential to its operation. This serves three purposes: (1) It will make your company run more efficiently; (2) it can raise the value and thus the sell price of your company, because buyers love businesses that don't depend on keeping the owners happy after the sale; and (3) it gives you time to accept your inevitable departure on your terms.

Here's the bottom line: It's not your problem anymore if the new owner runs it into the ground. Keep in mind that your old business was great, but that was then and this is now.

Hang around. If you're thinking of leaving the business immediately after the sale, consider staying a while instead. It will do you good to see that the company you're leaving is in good hands and will thrive, or that it's in different hands and moving in another direction. Either way, it will help you let go more effectively. Yes, you'll probably find this frustrating at times, and so will your former employees, but hang in there and help your people make the tough but necessary adaptations. It will help you, too.

Acknowledge that your business is gone. Don't fool yourself; the moment you sell your business, it will change. The buyer might have told you it plans to keep everything the same, but it's pretty rare that this actually happens. Things might get better, or they might get worse, but they will almost never remain the same. Do what you can to protect yourself and your employees after the sale (see chapter 12), but don't lose sleep over things you can't change. You certainly want the business to do well and your old employees to thrive, and if you stay in the business you will no doubt work tirelessly to see that it happens, but here's the bottom line: It's not your problem anymore if the new owner runs it into the ground. Keep in mind that your old business was great, but that was then and this is now. Now it becomes another business—a new business that might be even better.

Change your routine. After I sold my first business, but about a year before I left, I was able to relocate my office from Chicago's suburbs to downtown. This move helped me make the adjustment by breaking my accustomed routine; I had to commute to a different place and wouldn't even be passing by my old office anymore. You probably won't have this option, but there are other things you can do to get the same benefit: Change your hours, delegate responsibilities, change your parking space, eat at a different time or place—anything to break the routine you've followed for years before the sale. You'll be surprised at how these little changes can make a big difference in letting you move on.

Appoint a new leader. Before the sell process begins—or even after, if it's okay with the buyer—name a new president or leader and take a new title. I appointed a new president and took the chairman position for about a year before I left. This helped me keep a foot in the business and mentor the new leader without the demands of the profit-and-loss responsibility. It also helped my employees, who were loyal to me and knew I always looked out for them. It would have been tougher for them if I had just left without grooming a successor (see chapter 13).

Plan your next step. Don't just say, "I'll figure it out later," then walk away. Even if you're exhausted and just want a year off to do absolutely nothing, at least think about how you might be spending your post-company time. Yes, you'll take that well-deserved rest, but what will you do the second week? Work the "honey do" list? Hang out with your working friends? Travel? Set up a charity? Visualize your future; imagine yourself doing these things day after day. Can a person who enjoys the rough and tumble of the game be happy on the sidelines? If you begin having doubts, make some adjustments.

Swap horses in mid-gallop. Remember how we started off chapter 14 ("The 'Yak Yak' Factor") talking about the danger of switching horses in mid-gallop? It's especially hazardous if one of them is a slow horse (retiring, relaxing, recuperating) and the other one's fast (your company). But if they're both fast and both going in the same direction (building a business), the transition is a bit less tricky. Let's say you've decided to pursue another venture and can manage to do so without compromising your commitment to your buyer. You can use some of the transition time to work on the new idea so you can step right into it when you leave. I wanted to write a book; I had ten years' worth of proprietary notes, worksheets, and formulas to organize. I used the odd hours to start consolidating my notes, which enabled me to slide casually onto the second horse immediately after my last day. This helped me head off the blues.

CHAPTER 19

The Last Word

THE END IS HERE. You've read the book, re-examined your business, and completed the worksheets. Now you're ready to go forth and claim your best price. Right? Not so fast. Before you plunge headlong into the arena, here are a few parting words of advice:

Check your business pulse. Revisit the Max Value Model at the end of the Introduction. You should be proud to see how your Max Value Quotient has soared into the "proceed" area. But if your business still hasn't scored 200 or above, go back to the areas where you scored low and work to build those scores until you're in the go zone.

Start now. Whether you've been approached by a potential buyer, have just begun thinking about selling, or are serious about checking out—*get started!* The more time you have to devote to the effort, the better.

Stay the course. The process of selling a business is often a long one. Try to keep a steady course by managing the highs and lows. Keep your eye on the prize, and remember: You have a great plan, a proven plan, and it will work.

Visualize. Close your eyes and picture each upcoming meeting, each presentation, each interaction. I used to do this at night as

I was falling asleep—mostly because I couldn't help myself—but whenever you do it, it really works. Later, you may even experience déjà vu as you discover that each event goes pretty much the way you envisioned it.

Sell. Divesting yourself of your company is probably the biggest sale you've ever attempted. The stakes are high; pulling it off can set you up for life. Never forget that you're selling. Follow the same principles you would in selling any other large item.

Respect the process. Now that you know the drill, you are armed to use the sell process as an advantage, but don't forget that it is a process. Use the material discussed in the book to see around the corner; know what's coming, be ready for it, and pounce on it.

Don't get discouraged. You now have all the tools you need to succeed at this effort and to reach the goals and objectives you set when you started reading the book. Fear of the unknown should not be a factor.

Hit the website. Visit *www.stevekaplanlive.com* and click on the freebies button in the top navigation bar to find free materials that you'll find helpful across a variety of business disciplines.

Thanks for reading *Sell Your Business for the Max.* I wrote the book to help people like you, people who have worked tirelessly to reach their dreams. It gives me a chance to give back to a world that has been good to me by helping others succeed. Now, enough reading—get out there and sell for the max!

About the Author

Steve Kaplan has made a career out of shepherding businesses to success and helping others do the same. Turning Sampling Corporation of America (SCA), a basement operation, into a $250-million, thirteen-hundred-employee marketing company spanning sixteen countries was only the beginning. Over the past twenty years, he has helped more than one hundred businesses of all sizes and industries get big customers, restructure themselves, improve efficiency, boost morale, expand into new markets, and evaluate exit strategies, among other things. Recently he has been managing partner in a venture specializing in providing equity and operating strategy to a range of businesses.

As an expert entrepreneur, Steve has been recognized by *Inc.* magazine as a finalist for Entrepreneur of the Year and has won the Mercury Excellence Award in employee motivation. He has been the subject of many interviews and profiles at home and abroad in such media as *Advertising Age, Crain's Business, Food & Beverage, Selling, Target Marketing,* and the *Chicago Tribune.* His business practices have been featured in several college textbooks.

A graduate of Bradley University in Peoria, Illinois, he received his MBA from Rosary Graduate School of Business in River Grove, Illinois. He is a sought-after public speaker, presenting keynote speeches and workshops for businesses of all sizes. He has appeared on a variety of media (including CBS, NBC, Fox, and MSNBC) to discuss his experiences and insights. He has also written articles for several business magazines. He is a two-time *New York Times, Wall Street Journal, BusinessWeek,* and *USA Today* bestselling author.

Steve's vision and leadership made BountySCA Worldwide one of the world's leading marketing-service, database, and media organizations. He was a member of the executive committee of EuroRSCG, a 176-company conglomerate, and is the founder of Steve Kaplan Live (*www.stevekaplanlive.com*), a company providing packaged tools and consulting advice across a variety of business disciplines. He is the owner of the investment group Kaplan Enterprises LLC and a partner in eSkape, a sixty-thousand-square-foot Chicago-area family entertainment center.

Steve believes that both business *and* life should be an adventure and that both should be pursued with passion and vigor. Some of the adventures Steve has been fortunate enough to experience include scuba diving with hammerhead sharks off the Galapagos Islands and Cocoa Island, and whale sharks off Chale Island, Kenya; running with the bulls in Pamplona, Spain; ski-launched paragliding in Verbier, France; bungee jumping; gorilla trekking in the Congo; white-water rafting; hot-air ballooning over the Masai Mara, Kenya; body sledging in New Zealand; and rappelling down the waterfalls in Costa Rica.

Acknowledgments

A BIG THANK YOU TO

Jeff Morris for the great editing work on this, our third book together. It keeps getting better.

Josefina Manauta for your smart input, your creativity, and for keeping me focused on the task at hand. You and Descubrir are one of a kind.

Peter Workman for supporting my vision of sharing my knowledge with the business community.

Susan Bolotin for your creative input and leadership.

Team Workman for the great job on the book from A to Z.

Michael Solomon for the nice finishing touches and solid editing. It was a pleasure to work with you.

Jim Levine and everyone at The Levine Greenberg Agency.

Notes

Notes

Notes

Notes

Notes

Notes

Notes